God, Do You Care?

God, Do You Care?

DR. LYNDA HUNTER

W PUBLISHING GROUP™

www.wpublishinggroup.com

A Division of Thomas Nelson, Inc.
www.ThomasNelson.com

Published by W. Publishing Group, a division of Thomas Nelson, Inc., PO Box 141000, Nashville, Tennessee 37214, in association with the literary agency of Alive Communications, Inc., 7680 Goddard Street, Suite 200, Colorado Springs, Colorado 80920.

Unless otherwise indicated, Scripture quotations used in this book are from The Holy Bible, New International Version (NIV). Copyright 1973, 1978, 1984, International Bible Society. Used by permission of Zondervan Bible Publishers.

Other Scripture references are from the following sources:

The King James Version of the Bible (KJV).

The New King James Version (NKJV) copyright 1979, 1980, 1982, Thomas Nelson, Inc., Publishers.

New American Standard Bible (NASB) copyright 1960, 1977 by the Lockman Foundation.

Printed in the United States of America

01 02 03 04 05 06 PHX 9 8 7 6 5 4 3 2

In *My Utmost for His Highest,* Oswald Chambers writes: "The author who benefits you most is not the one who tells you something you did not know before, but the one who gives expression to the truth that has been dumbly struggling in you for utterance." May you find utterance in *God, Do You Care?*

Contents

Introduction

In April 1995, I stood in the congregation singing the song "Give Thanks" during a morning worship service. I loved the words, and I sang them with gusto. Then I mouthed the next part. "And now, let the weak say I am strong . . ."

I stopped singing. I knew the Joel 3:10 Bible reference from memory. Tears stung my eyes, however, as I began to think about my thirteen-year-old daughter. I'd been concerned about her behavior for a few months and had prayed for her often. The words of the song about the weak and the poor brought my fears to the surface, and I prayed for her once again as the singing continued around me.

The following November, I climbed into the car and headed for my daughter's school. My work in Christian ministry as editor of Focus on the Family's *Single-Parent Family* magazine seemed a mockery at that moment, as I drove through the winter streets for the third conference with her teachers at their request. Her grades had dropped from nearly straight As to Ds and Fs, and the teachers' comments discouraged me even more:

"She's become streetwise."

"She's hanging around with the wrong kinds of kids."

"She shows no respect to adults."

By the following March, things had deteriorated and the two younger siblings were being greatly affected. I gave their older sister an ultimatum: "Straighten up, or go live with your dad." At the principal's recommendation, straightening up would mean withdrawing the girls from their current school and enrolling them in a Christian school.

My older daughter left that weekend and moved some twelve hundred miles away to live with her non-Christian father.

I'd known my share of pain in life, including family illness, my father's death, and divorce some ten years before; but nothing could have prepared me for the pain I now experienced. My child, for whom I would give my life, appeared to turn her back on everything we'd stood for.

Weeks of desperation followed. I felt as though I'd failed as I mentally traveled *back* through the years trying to decide what I'd done wrong. I felt alone as I searched *around me* in vain for someone to help. I felt panicky as I looked at what lay *ahead.* And then I looked *up*.

After fasting two days, I managed to arrange some time off by myself, and I made my way into the mountains. I stopped for an early lunch and a trip through an outdoor mall, as I ached from places I didn't know I had. Later that afternoon, I arrived at my destination—the empty apartment I had borrowed from a friend.

I unloaded my luggage, then the real time of unloading began. I sat on the living room couch, put an empty chair across from me, and imagined God sitting there. I needed for Him to feel tangible to me that night. As I recounted each area of struggle, I asked, "What did I do wrong?" "Why have You allowed all this to happen to us? "Where do we go from here?" "God, do You care?"

When I'm asked about my greatest life lesson, I think of a variation of a bumper sticker I've seen: "Stuff happens." Somewhere else I read, "Life is hard, and then you die."

If we're alive, we know suffering. Some pain hurts worse than others, and it happens to everyone to some degree. But that's little consolation when the pain belongs to us.

The pain belonged to a crippled man in Acts 3. He woke up one morning the same way he had every day since his birth, unable to walk. He didn't know what it was like not to suffer. He struggled as always to get dressed and go to the same place as always to beg for the same thing as always. Temporary provision. *Maybe I'll get enough for two loaves of bread today and maybe a fish.* After all, some days were better than others. Disciples Peter and John probably also expected another ordinary day. But Jesus had recently left them, and their first miracle since His ascension into heaven was about to take place.

The man asked Peter and John for his pittance. If Peter had had pockets, he may have turned them wrong-side-out as he said, "Silver and gold I do not have, but what I have I give you" (Acts 3:6).

Alllll right, the man might have thought as he extended his cup.

"In the name of Jesus Christ of Nazareth, walk," Peter said (v. 6).

The crippled man's curiosity caused him to slip his right hand into the extended hand of the stranger. *What's he doing now? Doesn't he know I was born suffering? I can't stand up.*

But that's just what he did. An unfamiliar strength surged through his feet and ankles. He slid his right foot forward. It held his weight. Then his left foot. He walked! Slowly, then more quickly. He jumped and followed the two strangers into the temple where he praised their God. Next he went out and told everyone what had happened to him. Accustomed to perpetual suffering, he'd come expecting little but he got a lot. He'd come expecting a day's supply, but he got the supplies for a lifetime.

And now let the weak say I am strong and the poor say I am rich. Let the cripple say, "I can walk."

As I began to plan this book, I found lots of desperate personal experiences to share from my contact with life for forty-eight years—trials, heartaches, disappointments, suffering. I have worked through one hard place, only to go headlong into the next in my roles as woman, wife, and mother. In addition, many years of ministry through the magazine, radio, books, and speaking to people hurt by life reminded me of the inevitability of pain. I have heard pastor and author Charles Stanley say that when he wanted to present a sermon with which every member of the congregation would identify, he always chose the subject of suffering.

Yet I, along with countless others, have come to discover truth in the song I'd sung that March day, that weakness could be turned to strength and poverty to wealth. Why? Because of what the Lord has done.

And that's what this book is about. It's my effort as a fellow sufferer to help people who, in their pain, ask fundamental questions that get down to the foundation of life. The weak and the poor. The sick and the sorrowing. The sad and the hurting. You and me. This book is about pain, problems, and disappointments in life—yours and mine, big and small, catastrophic as well as everyday inconveniences. It's about suffering in all of us.

I may not be able to give a satisfactory explanation for why some things happen. But I can help you find hope, peace, and a future. I can help you grow and become a stronger person through an empathetic, passionate exploration of divine action in the midst of terrible human pain. My goal is to get down and examine pain from the bottom up and understand this inevitable condition from God's perspective. What can we as Christians do to both understand and come through life's challenges victoriously? How can we learn to measure life by its depth rather than by its length, by its promises rather than its problems?

I don't intend to defend God, nor will I offer academic or theological answers. Many good books already do that. Instead, I want to help you find hope somewhere beneath the rubble of your life, so that you may grow spiritually as you engage in those struggles. I also don't want to minimize the horribleness of suffering, tragedy, and pain, but to teach you to develop a template for looking inside your life at the difficulties you're experiencing, and then outside at what God is doing *in, through,* and *because* of these circumstances. In doing this, you won't spend so much time wondering *about* what's happening to you again. While you cannot control what you go through, you can control how you respond. This book will show you how to make the best for eternity out of what you're experiencing right now by examining the Bible's treatment of sufferings:

1. Perspective
2. Problem
3. Process
4. Purpose
5. Provision
6. Progress
7. Prayer
8. Preparation
9. People
10. Payoff

My daughter lived with her dad for the next four years. Many things happened during that time, but this book is not about what happened to her. Instead, *God, Do You Care?* is about what happened to her mom through that difficulty—how she grew, what she learned.

Perhaps you opened this book today expecting to get just another pittance in the bottom of your cup, as did the man at the temple gate. What you can get, instead, is strong feet and ankles not just for today's struggles, but also for those that lie ahead. Perhaps you aren't experiencing any difficulties at this phase of your life. But get ready. Sooner or later, the pain will be yours. A few months ago my friend Vickie didn't feel much pain. Then I received a call that her husband of more than thirty years had collapsed, and examination revealed an inoperable brain tumor. Once again, tragedy shattered the calm rhythm of life. Vickie's husband died before I could finish writing this book.

Missionary to India Amy Carmichael wrote:

> Life is like that. In an earthquake, it takes only seconds for a person who is just fine to be buried under the concrete of a collapsed parking facility or trapped in a building that has gone down like a house of cards. The same intensity of movement that can move mountains can also change lives in seconds. As one woman who had lost everything said: "Everything was fine—until yesterday."
>
> In everyday life too, when the mountains are not shaking, devastation can come just as speedily. Just when a person is at a peak of productivity, a medical diagnosis can pronounce a death sentence. A drunk going over the line on a curving mountain road can wipe out a whole family. A letter, a phone call, a knock at the door can change the entire course of a life. (Elizabeth R. Skoglund, *Amma: The Life and Words of Amy Carmichael,* Baker, 1994)

We will all experience pain, tragedy, and disappointment. But we don't have to be beggars or cripples. You and I can run and jump and praise God, and show those looking on how to do the same—in the midst of our suffering—because of what the Lord has done. Let's take the journey together and find out how.

When heaven is about to confer a great office on a man it always first exercises his mind and soul with suffering, and his body to hunger, and exposes him to extreme poverty, and baffles all his undertaking. By these means it stimulates his mind, hardens his nature, and enables him to do acts otherwise not possible to him.

—MENCIUS, THE CHINESE SAGE

CHAPTER 1

The Perspective

Do not be surprised at
the painful trial you are
suffering, as though
something strange were
happening to you. But
rejoice that you partici-
pate in the sufferings of
Christ, so that you may
be overjoyed when his
glory is revealed.

—1 PETER 4:12–13

Gretchen grew up going to a Catholic school in Illinois. At age nineteen, she married a handsome twenty-three-year-old boy from down the street, and they had two sons, Stanley and Howard, eleven months apart. Then Vietnam took Gretchen's husband away and returned a different man with a drug addiction. In 1974 their marriage ended, and Gretchen's former husband dropped out of sight. She lived with her parents for a time and found only part-time work at a phone company making sixty-four dollars a week. She and her sons started attending a Presbyterian church with her parents, where Gretchen taught Sunday school.

In 1981 Gretchen married Chuck, publisher of the town newspaper, whom, Gretchen says, "the boys took to like a cat to milk." Chuck's job changed while Stanley and Howard were in high school, and they moved to a new town in Illinois. This relocation, while financially beneficial, proved difficult for the boys. Stanley had trouble in school and got involved with alcohol. "Howard disconnected with us and hung around with undesirable people," Gretchen says. "He was always angry."

Gretchen struggled for help and fellowship through these trying times. She found a Spirit-filled church, which embraced her and became like family. Stanley graduated from high school, joined the Navy, and headed for San Diego. Howard finished high school the next year with straight As, and he enrolled in a nearby college where he made the dean's list. Then Chuck lost his job, and he and Gretchen moved to North Carolina.

Again Gretchen struggled. Again she searched for a church and extended family. Again she found it. "I started out Catholic," she says with a laugh, "then became Presbyterian, then Spirit-filled, then Baptist."

On January 8, 1992, Gretchen called to talk to Stanley after not hearing from him for several days. His roommate answered. "I've been trying to reach you. Stanley was killed this morning." Gretchen learned that while making his way to the military base on his motorcycle that morning, her older son had miscalculated his distance in passing a truck and was thrown under the wheels of the other vehicle.

Gretchen, Chuck, and Howard met Stanley's body, which the Navy had shipped to Illinois. After the funeral, Howard left the college he attended and went to North Carolina to help his mother deal with her grief. Soon after, a box arrived with Stanley's belongings. Howard claimed his brother's pea jacket.

Howard checked into continuing his education and got a part-time job at a convenience store. One night he put on Stanley's pea jacket and headed out the door for work. "I love you," Gretchen told her son.

"I love you too," Howard said.

Gretchen never saw him alive again. At work, two young men came into the store and stole fifty dollars just before unloading six bullets into Howard. And Gretchen buried her second son eleven weeks after burying the first.

Suffering—Universal, Inescapable

Tragedy, sorrow, affliction, suffering—the universal, inescapable facts of our human condition. In his book *The Life God Blesses* (Thomas Nelson, 1994), Gordon MacDonald calls unanticipated events we would choose to avoid, such as those that happened to Gretchen, "disruptive moments." They can be defined as enduring pain, misery, or difficulty. Suffering disrupts our inner tranquillity through emotional, physical, mental, and spiritual circumstances. Suffering brings pain, separation, and incompleteness. It can make us powerless and mute and push us toward hopelessness and despair. Suffering can maim, wither, or cripple the heart.

> *Suffering affects every aspect of our experience as human beings and unites people from every walk of life into a common experience of pain, irrespective of race or language, wealth or poverty, learning or virtue.*

Suffering affects every aspect of our experience as human beings and unites people from every walk of life into a common experience of pain, irrespective of race or language, wealth or poverty, learning or virtue. You can't know the right person or have the right things to avoid pain. Pain can't be bought or sold.

Whether the pain is as tragic and sudden as Gretchen's, or as slow and insidious as a bad marriage or a struggle with depression, suffering has no regard for merit or demerit, reward or punishment, honor or corruption. Like sun and rain, pain comes uninvited to the just and unjust alike, as we read in Matthew 5:45: "He causes his sun to rise on the evil and the good, and sends rain on the righteous and the unrighteous."

For hundreds of years, world religions have addressed and attempted to explain suffering. The first noble truth for Buddha is, "All life is suffering." The Talmud, teachings of rabbis between the years 200 B.C. and A.D. 500, describes the way Abraham faced testing:

> If you go to the marketplace, you will see the potter hitting his clay pots with a stick to show how strong and solid they are. But the wise potter hits only the strongest pots, never the flawed ones. God sends such tests and afflictions only to people He knows are capable of handling them, so that they and others can learn the extent of their spiritual strength.

The Bible also contains countless stories about men and women whose lives portrayed the inevitability of suffering. Daniel thrown in the lions' den. Shadrach, Meshach, and Abednego left to die in the fiery furnace. Joseph locked in prison. Moses stuck on the backside of the desert. Esther facing possible death for defending her people. Abigail trapped in a marriage with an evil man. All of Jesus' disciples died a martyr's death.

Jesus suffered too. In many Bible commentaries, He's even called the "suffering servant." But if Jesus took on pain for us, why do we have to experience affliction? Philip Yancey writes in *Open Windows:* "Jesus' death is the cornerstone of the Christian faith . . . Jesus in a sense dignified pain. Of all the kinds of lives he could have lived, he chose a suffering one" (Crossway, 1982). Author Dorothy Sayers wrote: "For whatever reason God chose to make man as he is—limited and suffering and subject to sorrows and death—He had the honesty and courage to take His own medicine" (quoted in *The Quoteable Christian,* Barbour, 1988).

If Christ Himself could not avoid suffering, as Christians we're not exempt from these difficulties either. In *Table Talk* (Keats, 1979), Martin Luther wrote: "Our suffering is not worthy the name of suffering. When I consider my crosses, tribulations, and temptations, I shame myself almost to death thinking what are they in comparison of the sufferings of my blessed Savior Jesus Christ."

Our faith could even make us a special target for enemy attack. I spoke with Isabel one year after she gave her heart to Christ. She didn't report perfect circumstances. Instead she said, "It's been the hardest year of my life." One night when I was a little girl, my family took a man to church with us, and that night he prayed the sinner's prayer. On our way home, my mom told him, "Be prepared, your troubles are just beginning. But now, you have someone to go with you through them."

I felt afraid while listening to my mother speak these words to the man, afraid that she would scare him off. What did my mom know that I had yet to learn?

When It's *Your* Pain . . .

There's nothing we can do to prevent pain no matter who we are, and God promises us He will go with us through it. Why, then, do we squirm when we face hardship? Why do we ask: "Why?" "Will I ever be happy again?" "How will this fit together for my good?" "How could a good God allow . . . ?" "God, do You care?"

Our natural inclination as human beings is to search for the reasons why things happen. When I faced the difficulties with my daughter, I thought about how I had tried to be a good person. Right in the sight of God. Living in a more godly fashion than most people I knew. Doing God's work. All my parenting had been deliberate. Other people who didn't invest nearly the effort I had had kids who had turned out OK. But I found that reading the

Scriptures and realizing their truths were two different things when I ached in the depths of my very soul or cried with others who hurt.

Because of pain's paradoxical nature, we find it hard to understand. It is both inevitable and alien to us. As a result, some of us respond positively to pain, others react negatively. We protect ourselves and our family against pain, and our questions become attempts to find assurance that an order to reality that transcends our problems actually does exist and that everything will be OK.

We're not the first generation to ask God questions about our suffering. Because of the many difficulties the Israelites encountered, in Numbers 14:2–3, they questioned why they ever had to leave Egypt in search of the Promised Land. The books of Jeremiah and Lamentations in the Bible are filled with questions about the Israelites' Babylonian captivity. Even Jesus asked of God, "Why have you forsaken me?" (Matthew 27:46).

> *So there comes a point when our* why *questions need to turn into* how*? "How do I work my way through?" "How can I grow through this thing?" "How can you use this trial in my life to help others?" "How can I become more like Christ?"*

God allows our questions—for a while. He even answers some of these questions. We read in Deuteronomy 29:29 how God reveals some hidden things while He keeps others a mystery to the human mind. "The secret things belong to the LORD our God, but the things revealed belong to us and to our children forever, that we may follow all the words of this law." By getting to know the mind of God, we can understand some of why and how He's using our trying circumstances. But no matter how earnest our prayers, penetrating or intelligent our inquiries this side of heaven, we'll never know all the reasons why we suffer.

So there comes a point when our *why* questions need to turn into *how?* "How do I work my way through?" "How can I grow through this thing?" "How can you use this trial in my life to help others?" "How can I become more like Christ?" W. C. Fields once said, "There comes a time in the affairs of humanity when you must take the bull by the tail and face the situation." Asking the *how* questions helps you face the situation.

A Change in Perspective

The key to switching your questions from *why?* to *how?* involves a change in perspective. Finding ways to not only accept suffering, but also to find meaning in it or to live through and beyond it involves a deliberate effort to change the way you view the bad things that happen to you. The Bible urges us to implant a future perspective into our present. This allows us to separate the lasting, eternal results from the temporary inconvenience they cause.

In Mark 1:16–20, Jesus challenged Simon (later called Peter) and his brother, Andrew, to change their perspective from one that focused on catching fish for the day to one that valued catching souls for eternity. "At once they left their nets and followed him" (v. 18). Simon's and Andrew's lives were changed forever, because they dared to alter their perspective. In the same way, what we do with our suffering—how we respond—depends on our perspective. When we glance back, pain can fade like the distant memory of a difficult childbirth; we often forget the pain and only the results survive. The good things that come out of suffering can remain like steppingstones above raging water. They carry us to the other side of suffering. One experience with pain can prepare us for the next. This enables us to move confidently forward to whatever lies ahead.

And that difference comes as a result of our perspective of God. We can trust God or not trust Him through the hard places. Affliction either warms the person up toward spiritual things or turns her cold. We can become better or bitter.

Accept that pain will come, then move on. "Life is difficult," writes M. Scott Peck on the first page of his book *The Road Less Traveled* (Simon & Schuster, 1978). He goes on to say: "This is a great truth, one of the greatest truths. It is a great truth because once we truly see this truth, we transcend it. Once we truly know that life is difficult—once we truly understand and accept it—then life is no longer difficult. Because once it is accepted, the fact that life is difficult no longer matters."

Webster defines perspective as the capacity to view things in their true relations or relative importance and to view your own task in a larger framework. Peter sought to take the subject of suffering and offer Christians a different way of viewing it. He wrote 1 Peter to Christians living in various parts of Asia Minor who suffered rejection in the world because of their obedience to Christ. Daily trials such as illness, divorce, and death had been compounded with Jesus' crucifixion. Instead of dwelling on these unfortunate circumstances, Peter offered Christians a higher view, a heavenly view. He offered them a change of perspective:

> Do not be surprised at the painful trial you are suffering, as though something strange were happening to you. But rejoice that you participate in the sufferings of Christ, so that you may be overjoyed when his glory is revealed. (1 Peter 4:12–13)

Peter—a fellow sufferer who walked with Christ, then lost Him in person only to find Him through the Holy Spirit—ultimately died a martyr's death. He was telling us, Don't be surprised, bad stuff's gonna happen. You're not the only one who goes through hard places. Then he admonished us to be joyous and look forward to what lies ahead in the eternal. What? Be joyous? Look ahead? It's all I can do to get through today!

Another time, we read how Peter took a different perspective on a bad situation, only this time it wasn't the disciple Peter, but Peter Rabbit from the well-known children's book by Beatrix Potter (Penguin, 1989). Peter's mother had instructed her four children not to go to Mr. McGregor's garden. Three of the children complied, but Peter went straight to the forbidden garden and squeezed under the gate.

Peter ate lettuce, beans, and radishes, then parsley to soothe his full stomach. But his feast quickly ended when, at the cucumber frame, he met Mr. McGregor and a chase ensued. We read: "Peter was most dreadfully frightened. He rushed all over the garden for he had forgotten the way back to the gate." He lost a shoe in the potatoes and got caught by his large jacket buttons in a gooseberry net. Then he heard the call to change his perspective: "Peter gave himself up for lost and shed big tears; but his sobs were overheard by some friendly sparrows, who flew to him in great excitement and implored him to exert himself."

Though Peter's particular suffering happened as the result of his wrong decision, he encountered a run for his life. The sparrows had encouraged him to change the way he looked at things and then to find fresh energy to carry on. So Peter "climbed upon a wheelbarrow and peeped over." From that vantage point, Peter was able to see more than the tangled morass around him. Rather, he got a clear view of where he'd come from, where the enemy was, and where he needed to go. Peter jumped down, headed for the gate, and slipped underneath. "He never stopped running or looked behind him till he got home to the big fir tree."

Though this children's book presents a somewhat unconventional way to view a change in perspective, disciple Peter and Peter Rabbit offered much the same advice: You're going to have some rough places. Climb above your circumstances, take a good look, get your direction, and then keep going—until you reach home.

Bible

We can read about three men from the Bible who also climbed upon their wheelbarrows and dared to change their perspective:

Job

Job suffered boils over his body and lost vocation, home, cattle, seven sons, and three daughters. He cried out, "Even today my complaint is bitter; his hand is heavy in spite of my groaning" (Job 23:2).

This man knew what it was like to suffer. "If only I knew where to find him; if only I could go to his dwelling! I would state my case before him and fill my mouth with arguments. I would find out what he would answer me, and consider what he would say" (Job 23:3–5).

Job might have prayed one more time to what appeared to be a deaf ear: "But if I go to the east, he is not there; if I go to the west, I do not find him. When he is at work in the north, I do not see him; when he turns to the south, I catch no glimpse of him." (Job 23:8–9).

Then something changed—not in his circumstances, but in Job's heart. He spoke with fresh faith: "But he knows the way that I take; when he has tested me, I will come forth as gold" (Job 23:10).

We read further in this book of the Bible how God heard His

servant's prayer and restored him. Job discarded all the theories offered to him, and in the end he accepted his suffering. He never did find a rational explanation, but he saw in God a certainty that overcame his doubts and tears. The certainty didn't come that day, but the change in Job did, and that presented a pathway through which God could work.

David

The Bible calls David a man after God's heart (1 Samuel 13:14). Yet he walked through deep valleys and looked for God from there: "I cried out to God for help; I cried out to God to hear me. When I was in distress, I sought the LORD; at night I stretched out untiring hands and my soul refused to be comforted. I remembered you, O God, and I groaned; I mused, and my spirit grew faint" (Psalm 77:1–3).

David found himself lost in despair. He searched everywhere for answers from God: "You kept my eyes from closing; I was too troubled to speak. I thought about the former days, the years of long ago; I remembered my songs in the night. My heart mused and my spirit inquired: 'Will the Lord reject forever? Will he never show his favor again? Has his unfailing love vanished forever? . . . Has God forgotten to be merciful? Has he in anger withheld his compassion?'" (Psalm 77:4–9).

Notice the personal pronouns David uses. Twenty times in the first six verses he loaded his prayer with words like *I, my, me, mine.*

But then it happened. David remembered God's faithfulness: "Your ways, O God, are holy. What god is so great as our God? You are the God who performs miracles; you display your power among the peoples. With your mighty arm you redeemed your people, the descendants of Jacob and Joseph" (Psalm 77:13–15).

David had rediscovered the source of his strength and power.

Jeremiah

Another man, Jeremiah, cried so much that he earned the nickname the "weeping prophet."

"I am the man who has seen affliction by the rod of his wrath. He has driven me away and made me walk in darkness rather than light: indeed, he has turned his hand against me again and again, all day long. He has made my skin and my flesh grow old and has broken my bones. He has besieged me and surrounded me with bitterness and hardship. He has made me dwell in darkness like those long dead" (Lamentations 3:1–6).

As long as Jeremiah dwelt on his troubles, everything seemed hopeless. Then like Job and David, Jeremiah's self-pity ceased, and he remembered whom he served.

Jeremiah goes on to blame God for walling him in, weighting him down, keeping him in darkness, barring his way, making his paths crooked, mangling him, and leaving him without hope. "I remember my affliction and my wandering, the bitterness and the gall. I well remember them, and my soul is downcast within me" (Lamentations 3:19–20).

As long as Jeremiah dwelt on his troubles, everything seemed hopeless. Then like Job and David, Jeremiah's self-pity ceased, and he remembered whom he served. "Yet this I call to mind and therefore I have hope: Because of the LORD's great love we are not consumed, for his compassions never fail. They are new every morning; great is your faithfulness. I say to myself, 'The LORD is my portion; therefore I will wait for him.' The LORD is good to those whose hope is in him, to the one who seeks him; it is good to wait quietly for the salvation of the LORD" (Lamentations 3:21–26).

Job, David, and Jeremiah made conscious decisions to look to God. They declared their faith in Him. They recalled His character.

They praised Him for His strength and ability to restore. When they did, things began to change.

Application

Stanley and Howard died on January 8 and March 24, 1992, respectively. Their deaths will never make sense, and Gretchen admits asking more than her share of questions to God after losing both her sons. She described to me how she responded when the policeman told her that her second son had died: "My son can't be dead, because I just buried a son. I'm never praying again, because [God] just takes them away. I don't understand any of it. I want to die."

But as time went on, Gretchen changed her perspective and found meaning in her sorrow. She told me recently,

> Suffering is something that is with you all the time. Under the surface of everything you do. In the pit of your stomach. But you don't have to stay with it. I've gotten through by not putting my focus on it [the suffering], but on God. What happened to me doesn't really belong to me. God is using it for something. I'd rather focus on Him, though I don't ignore that I'm in grief. I would rather give glory to the remembrance of my sons and to Jesus by not staying down with the suffering. By not getting beaten, Satan has not won. He has not taken away my faith.

Gretchen has learned that pain is inevitable, but wallowing is optional. And to prevent wallowing, she's learned how to change her perspective. What steps can you take to begin your deliberate efforts of changing your perspective?

DON'T . . .

Don't be surprised. Like Job, David, and Jeremiah, we find it easy to become consumed with self-pity when trouble strikes. But if we stay warned and prepared, we'll make it through. Suffering is going to happen to the believer as well as the unbeliever. Understand that, and don't be surprised or feel victimized when it comes. But also realize that if we're in Christ, we are *in Christ,* and nothing that comes along can destroy us. "We are hard pressed on every side, but not crushed; perplexed, but not in despair; persecuted, but not abandoned; struck down, but not destroyed" (2 Corinthians 4:8–9). God is our buffer who will take the hard hits that will ultimately come.

Don't bemoan others' better fortunes. Remember when Peter asked Jesus about His plans for John's future? Jesus responded, "'If I want him to remain alive until I return, what is that to you? You must follow me'" (John 21:22). As people, we find it easy to look at others and think they have it easier or are finding better fortune than we are. They aren't, because even if they aren't suffering today, they will in some form or another. But we must also resist going to the other extreme and feeling better because someone else feels worse. We can be thankful for our blessings, but we need to come alongside others when they're going through hard times. Then when it's our turn, God will provide the same for us. Meanwhile, as Jesus told Peter, you must just keep following Him.

Don't worry that God won't see you through. The Bible tells us about the unalterable attributes of God in James 1:17. Circumstances change, but God doesn't. He's the same yesterday, today, and forever (Hebrews 13:8). If yesterday God helped Daniel, Shadrach, Meshach, and Abednego; Joseph, Moses, Esther, and Abigail; Job, Jeremiah, and David through their suffering, He'll help you and me today and in the trials that lie ahead. God does not change.

Don't look other places. God is the answer. You'll face the temptation to listen to other people as Job did at first, who offer wrong advice, unfounded in Scripture. Books also abound with information about how to deal with disappointment and sorrow, but many will not bring you closer to God.

Do . . .

Do find ways to look outside yourself. Be certain that there's a bigger purpose to your suffering than you feel in your own discomfort. I heard a quote once about someone who bemoaned her plight. A wise person heard these complaints and said, "There's nothing wrong with you that a good look around a hospital won't cure." While going through hard places, we can always find someone who's got it better. But we can always, always find those who have it worse. Far worse. The life-changing kind of worst. When I taught fifth grade, I went to the office one day after school to call my beautician cousin to schedule a haircut. "My hair's driving me crazy," I said to my cousin. When I got off the phone, the secretary said with a sweet smile, "I know. Ever since I lost my hair in chemotherapy, this wig has been itching me to death." Find ways to look outside yourself.

Do rejoice and be thankful. No matter what's wrong, there's still lots right. Instead of dwelling on all the bad stuff, play a game with your child tonight and listen to the laughter. Phone a friend who's been close to you for a long time. Sing praise songs or read a psalm.

Do find ways to help others. Find people in your church or workplace or neighborhood who are going through trying circumstances. Bake them some cookies. Send them a card. Pay them a visit. Hug them. Tell them you're praying for them, and remember to do it every day.

Do look for the bigger picture. Acknowledge that you can't entirely see the big picture no matter how many wheelbarrows you crawl upon. But you've entrusted your life to Jesus Christ, who is all-knowing and all-seeing. And trust Him to see you through.

Do look forward to future rewards. Be sure you've asked Christ into your heart. Next be sure no unconfessed sin remains in your life today. Then pray. Express your desire to understand life through God's eyes in light of eternity. If you can do all this, you've set yourself up for a change in perspective.

Conclusion

Gretchen opened a skin-care salon some time back. She talks about how God sends people her way to hear her witness. One woman came in with dry eyelids, and when Gretchen asked why, the woman explained that her son had just died in an automobile accident. "We held hands and cried together and prayed countless times," Gretchen says.

Two young boys came to Christ as a result of Gretchen sharing her testimony with a congregation, and they remain in touch. "Whatever you give to the Lord, He gives back four hundredfold," Gretchen says. "Well, I get back eight hundred kids. I haven't kept track of their names. Sunday school, beauty college, Girl Scouts, Bible studies. They're all lining up out there. I don't know what will happen after I hit eight hundred. But I do know somebody's keeping count somewhere."

That's what I call a change of perspective.

Bible Study

God loves you, and He not only knows what you've been through, He knows what you're facing today and what lies ahead for tomorrow. But He doesn't just see these things as isolated situations. He sees problems as opportunities to make you more like Himself, so that you can grow and then help someone else that He also loves and knows. Someday, we'll all sit together in heaven and sing His praises. The pains will be long forgotten, but the lessons they taught us and the good they brought will remain, as we live forever with Him.

Meanwhile, live by promises of what will come, not by explanations of what is happening now. And use the mind that God has given you to seek guidance from His Word.

1. Is it OK to question God?

It's not only OK to question God, but He promises that He always hears and answers His children. His response, however, does not necessarily assure that He takes away our pain.

PSALM 34:4–7: "I sought the LORD, and he answered me; he delivered me from all my fears. Those who look to him ______ ______________; their faces are never covered with shame. This poor man called, and the LORD __________ him; he saved him out of all his troubles. The angel of the LORD encamps around those who fear him, and he ________________ them."

V. 10: "Those who seek the LORD lack no ________ thing."

V. 15: The eyes of the LORD are on the righteous and his ears are __________________ to their cry.

V. 17–20: "The righteous cry out, and the LORD hears them; he delivers them from all their ________________. The LORD is close to the brokenhearted and saves those who are crushed in spirit. A righteous man may have many troubles, but the LORD delivers him from them all; he

_______________ all his bones, not one of them will be _____________."

v. 22: "No one will be condemned who takes _____________ in him."

Is it OK to ask questions of God for a while?

____

2. Can a trial ever destroy me?

Christians live now for eternity. Because of that fact, the present doesn't seem so permanent and the future doesn't seem so remote. As a result of our eternity-boundedness, illnesses, accidents, murders, or natural disasters can destroy our bodies, but nothing can get to our souls. God will always go with us through hardship and bring us out safely on the other side in ways that bring Him glory.

ISAIAH 43:2: "When you pass through the waters, I will be _________ you; and when you pass through the rivers, they will not ___________ over you. When you walk through the fire, you will not be _____________; the flames will not set you ablaze. For I am the LORD, your God, the Holy One of Israel, your Savior."

Can a trial ever destroy you?

____

3. How does the Bible define pain?

Though Scripture doesn't specifically define pain, it refers to it in different analogies. All of them suggest hard places and, perhaps, speak to the reader in a way mere words could not:

- Storms

PSALM 69:1–2: "Save me, O God, for the ___________ have come up to my neck. I sink in the miry ___________, where there is no foothold. I have come into the deep waters; the ___________ engulf me."

- Warfare

JOB 19:11–12: "His anger burns against me; he counts me among his _____________. His ___________ advance in force; they build a siege ramp against me and ___________ around my tent."

JOB 6:4: "The ___________ of the Almighty are in me, my spirit drinks in their poison; God's _____________ are marshaled against me."

- Harvest

MATTHEW 3:12: "His _________________ fork is in his hand, and he will clear his threshing floor, gathering his _________ into the barn and burning up the chaff with unquenchable fire."

ISAIAH 63:3 : "I have _____________ the winepress alone; from the nations no one was with me. I trampled them in my anger and trod them down in my wrath; their blood spattered my garments, and I stained all my clothing."

- Birth

MATTHEW 24:7–8: "Nation will rise against nation, and kingdom against kingdom. There will be _____________ and _____________________ in various places. All these are the beginning of birth pains."

ROMANS 8:22–23: "We know that the whole creation has be groaning as in the pains of childbirth right up to the present time. Not only so, but we ourselves, who have the ________________________ of the Spirit, groan inwardly as we wait eagerly for our adoption as sons, the ______________________ of our bodies."

- Race

ISAIAH 40:31: "But those who hope in the LORD will renew their ________________. They will soar on wings like eagles; they will ______ and not grow weary, they will ________ and not be faint."

- Trials

JOB 9:29: "Since I am already found ____________, why should I struggle in vain?"
JOB 13:3: "But I desire to speak to the Almighty and to __________ my case with God."

What does your pain, or that of someone you know, feel like?
____

4. *How did Christ suffer?*

Though the Son of God, Jesus chose to suffer for our sakes. "He was a man of sorrow and acquainted with grief" (Isaiah 53:3). As a result, Jesus understands what we're going through. Isaiah 63:9 tells us that God identifies with His people when they hurt. God does not sit far removed from our pain, but He draws nearest to us when we seek Him, which most often happens during times of difficulty.

• Jesus suffered poverty and loneliness.
MATTHEW 26:56: "The disciples _______________ him [Jesus] and fled."

• Jesus suffered fatigue, hunger, pain, thirst, ill treatment, and rejection of family and friends.
JOHN 1:11: "He came to that which was his own, but his own did not _______________ him."

What are you feeling now that Jesus felt before you?
____
____

5. What did we gain as a result of Jesus' suffering besides eternal life?

You know how nice it is when you're hurting to talk to someone who understands? That's what we have with Jesus. You and I will never face anything that Jesus has not already faced.

HEBREWS 2:17–18: "For this reason he had to be made like his brothers in every way, in order that he might become a _______________ and _______________ high priest in service to God, and that he might make atonement for the sins of the people. Because he himself suffered when he was tempted, he is able to help those who are being tempted."

HEBREWS 4:14–16: "Therefore, since we have a great high priest who has gone through the heavens, Jesus the Son of God, let us hold firmly to the __________ we profess. For we do not have a high priest who is unable to

____________________ with our weaknesses, but we have one who has been tempted in every way, just as we are—yet was without sin. Let us then approach the throne of grace with confidence, so that we may receive mercy and find grace to help us in our time of need."

Because of Jesus, how can you benefit today? ____
____

6. *Why did Jesus suffer?*
   • To show a loving God.
   JOHN 14:9–10: "Anyone who has seen me has see the ___________. How can you say, 'Show us the Father'? Don't you believe that I am in the Father, and that the Father is in me?"

   • To identify with us.
   HEBREWS 2:18: "Because he himself ________________ when he was tempted, he is able to help those who are being tempted."

   How can you express your gratitude to Christ for what He did for you? __________________________________
   ____

7. *Will God comfort me through my trials?*
   You can always count on God for comfort through your trials if you are in Him. He uses His Word, other people, and various ways to talk to us.

PSALM 16:7–8: "I will praise the LORD, who counsels me; even at night my heart instructs me. I have set the LORD always before me. Because he is at my ___________ hand, I will not be ____________."

In what areas do you need comfort today?

____

8. *What benefit is there in suffering?*

The benefit comes through the big picture. You see glimpses of the results as you see yourself grow and become more like Christ. You'll see all the benefits one day when we get to heaven.

MATTHEW 5:10–12: "Blessed are those who are persecuted because of righteousness, for theirs is the kingdom of heaven. Blessed are you when people _____________ you, persecute you and falsely say all kinds of evil ____________ you because of me. Rejoice and be glad, because great is your ____________ in heaven, for in the same way they persecuted the prophets who were before you."

JOHN 15:18–19, 21: "If the ___________ hates you, keep in mind that it hated me first. If you belonged to the world, it would love you as its own. As it is, you do not belong to the world, but I have _____________ you out of the world. That is why the world hates you. . . . They will treat you this way because of my name, for they do not know the One who sent me."

ACTS 5:41: "So they departed from the presence of the council, rejoicing that they were counted _____________ to _____________ shame for His name (NKJV).

As you've begun the process of changing your perspective, what might God do with the discomforts you're experiencing?

Dear God:

I know that pain is going to come for all of us. And as people, we can choose to go through hardship with You or without You. Through Your strength or through the strength we muster on our own. I choose to go in Your strength. I realize that my walk with You might make me especially vulnerable to hardship. But show me how to change my perspective. Show me how to view suffering through Your eyes instead of mine, where You can see the past, present, and future clearly. Help me to not be surprised at the painful trials I suffer, as though something strange were happening to me. Help me rejoice that You participate in the sufferings with me. Help me remember that someday I will be overjoyed when Your glory is revealed. Meanwhile, help me stay on top of the wheelbarrow, and help me see things as You do. In the name of Jesus Christ, amen.

In perplexities—when we cannot tell what to do, when we cannot understand what is going on around us—let us be calmed and steadied and made patient by the thought that what is hidden from us is not hidden from Him.

—Frances Ridley Havergal

CHAPTER 2

The Problem

It is the glory of God to
conceal a matter; to
search out a matter is
the glory of kings.

—PROVERBS 25:2

My son, Clint, was to play in a Saturday-noon basketball game. He and I headed into town about 10:30 to run an errand before going to the gym. We had reached the edge of town when Clint announced that he had forgotten his basketball clothes, so I signaled for the nearest exit. We would have to work within a much tighter time frame now. My irritation at my son's neglect intensified when we caught the red light at the place we needed to make a U-turn before getting back onto the interstate. And a long red light it was. We waited and waited. Finally our turn came, and I accelerated toward the highway.

Soon we merged into traffic and into what appeared to be a cloud of dust, which loomed like a wall in front of us. I drove ahead several hundred feet and moved into the left lane. Then I saw the problem. A van had blown a tire from the southbound side of the road, crossed the median, and hit a small truck in front of us head-on. I pulled to a stop, the second vehicle to the scene, and I gasped at the bodies I saw strewn along the highway. I called 911 and waited to see if I could help. When emergency crews started arriving, I pulled into the grass, onto a service road in the median, and back toward town. The interstate remained closed for several hours. I later found out that seven people died in the collision, including a two-year-old child. The evening news announced free counseling services to those of us who had witnessed the atrocity. They told how one vehicle contained men returning home after finishing a job in a nearby town; the occupants in the other vehicle were planning a leisurely day at a Denver mall. Neither made it to their destinations.

I have a friend named Patrick, with whom I've worked in ministry. One day he dropped off his sixteen-year-old daughter, Lauren, at the airport. A wonderful opportunity had presented itself for Lauren to go to Paris to pursue her interest in clothing design. She would fly to New York, where she would board another flight to France. Patrick arrived home from the airport some distance away to his phone ringing. "Which airline did Lauren use? What was her flight number?"

The caller went on to explain that Paris-bound TWA Flight 800 had gone down in the ocean shortly after takeoff in New York. The likelihood of survivors remained slim. The TV news had already begun announcing the disaster, telling about the number of students aboard who were headed for Paris.

At last a nervous Patrick found Lauren's itinerary. With shaking hands he looked down at the print on the page. Flight TWA *900,* not TWA 800, that was Lauren's flight. It had taken off twelve minutes earlier for the same destination as the one now lost in the ocean.

Patrick called me soon after the incident. "For what seemed like an eternity," he said, "I didn't know if my daughter was dead."

I breathed a sigh of relief, and thanked God that He had spared one of the people on my prayer list. But what about those He didn't spare? What about the parent whose daughter was dead, who would never see that child grow up? If Clint and I had not caught the red light, we could well have been lying along the highway with the other victims. God spared us by only a few seconds. But what about those He didn't spare? Did God love them any less?

What's the Problem?

How does it happen that God spares some from tragedy while others go to an early death? Why does He heal one person and not another? Why do some have anything they want to eat while others starve? Why is one nation abundantly blessed and another cursed with misfortune?

We read in Luke 4:25–27 about all kinds of widows in Elijah's day and multitudes of people with leprosy in Elisha's day. Yet God sent Elijah to only one widow and Elisha to only one leper. Why? Hebrews 11 names men and women for whom God did great things as a result of their faith, including Abraham, Sarah, Abel, and Noah. But what caused a group of men and women to draw the short straw in Hebrews 11:35–38? They don't even get their names mentioned, yet the Bible applauds their courage and faith:

> Others were tortured and refused to be released . . . Some faced jeers and flogging, while still others were chained and put in prison. They were stoned; they were sawed in two; they were put to death by the sword. They went about in sheepskins and goatskins, destitute, persecuted and mistreated—the world was not worthy of them.

Why didn't God deliver these men and women who stood firm in their faith? Why the injustice? Or is it simply justice of a different kind, which we as human beings have trouble understanding? I maintain that the answer to all these questions lies with the sovereignty of God. But how does the phrase *God's sovereignty* become something other than a phrase used to explain everything we don't understand? How do we keep from reacting like a child when a parent says, "Because I said so," and doesn't bother to explain further reasons?

I titled this chapter "The Problem." Yet, as we discuss the problem, and as I explain that God is sovereign, in charge of all things, those two ideas appear to contradict each other. The problem lies in the way we look at things. While God has things figured out, we do not. While He can see the big picture, we cannot. While He knows exactly what's going on in this world, we do not. And that's the problem. Amy Carmichael wrote:

> Some issues will never be completely understood on earth. Rather than allowing those unanswered questions to disillusion us, they should actually increase our belief in a Divine Being; for if we understood the mind of God in its entirety, He would cease to be God or we ourselves would be God. By definition God is unknowable—if He is not, He is not God. Some aspect of the problem of pain we can only understand in heaven. Now, as we live on this earth, the ultimate answer is faith. Yet faith is not to be viewed as a second-best weapon for a problem for which we simply have no other solution. (Elizabeth R. Skoglund, *Amma: The Life and Words of Amy Carmichael,* Baker, 1994)

So what's the answer? Get to really know the character of God. Some things will still remain beyond our ability to understand. Others will be made clear as we get to know the One who created all things. A. W. Tozer writes, "There is scarcely an error in doctrine or a failure in applying Christian ethics that cannot be traced finally to imperfect and ignoble thoughts about God" *(The Knowledge of the Holy,* HarperSanFrancisco, 1992).

And replacing those ignoble thoughts about God with knowledge of His character comes as a result of a lifelong pursuit of God.

Knowing God

God's sovereignty: the supreme authority of God. He is not subject to any power or law that could be conceived as superior to Himself. A. W. Tozer defines God's sovereignty as the ability to rule the entire creation in an all-knowing, all-powerful way. He goes on to say:

> Were there even one datum of knowledge, however small, unknown to God, His rule would break down at that point. To be Lord over all the creation, He must possess all knowledge. And were God lacking one infinitesimal modicum of power, that lack would end His reign and undo His kingdom; that one stray atom of power would belong to someone else and God would be a limited ruler and hence not sovereign. *(The Knowledge of the Holy)*

God's sovereignty includes His absolute freedom to do whatever He pleases, without interference, to carry out His eternal plan. No one and no thing can hinder or stop Him. This gives God universal authority and freedom to do whatever He pleases, as we see in these verses:

> The race is not to the swift or the battle to the strong, nor does food come to the wise or wealth to the brilliant or favor to the learned; but time and chance happen to them all. (Ecclesiastes 9:11)

> In his heart a man plans his course, but the LORD determines his steps. (Proverbs 16:9)

> Many are the plans in a man's heart, but it is the LORD's purpose that prevails. (Proverbs 19:21)

> The king's heart is in the hand of the LORD; he directs it like a watercourse wherever he pleases. (Proverbs 21:1)

> The LORD said to him, "Who gave man his mouth? Who makes him deaf or mute? Who gives him sight or makes him blind? Is it not I, the LORD?" (Exodus 4:11)

> When a trumpet sounds in a city, do not the people tremble? When disaster comes to a city, has not the LORD caused it? (Amos 3:6)

> The lot is cast into the lap, but its every decision is from the LORD. (Proverbs 16:33)

You and I are said to be free individuals. Yet we are bound by everything from our physical, emotional, and psychological restraints to the laws of the universe. We operate freely only within the existing laws, but inherent within those laws is the presence of evil, suffering, and death. We don't know why God allowed the original sin, but we do know that He permits evil and its results in some areas of His creation for right now. He has a plan, unknown to us, and because God cannot lie, we have to trust that He knows what He's doing and that everything will be more than OK in the end.

But I believe there's a component in the Christian life that we often overlook and fail to take advantage of. Before Clint and I left our home that Saturday morning, we prayed, as our family has every day for the past fifteen years, for the whole armor from Ephesians 6: "Give us Your helmet of salvation and Your breastplate of righteousness. Gird our loins about with truth and shoe our feet with the gospel of peace. Give us the sword of the spirit, which is the Word of God and the shield of faith to quench all the fiery darts of the enemy."

With that prayer and a little breakfast, we went into town that morning and averted a near-death accident. I believe that was no coincidence. I also believe it was no coincidence that Lauren's life was spared. Patrick knew that after my daughter went to live with her dad, I had made a list of teenagers to pray for—seventy-four of them in all—and Lauren and her brother, John, were two of the names on that list. I believe my prayers, along with others, dispatched guardian angels to their sides and spared them from disaster.

Yes, God is sovereign. Only He knows if others were praying for the people who did die in those two mishaps. Because He is all-powerful and free to do whatever He wishes to bring about His purpose, that purpose may have been better accomplished through death, or in other cases, through sickness or bankruptcy. When we're in Christ, we can realize this principle and await the day when we will fully understand. When we don't, we're left trying to figure things out and blaming God for our misfortunes. I do know that those who knew God when they drew their last breath are spending eternity in a place where "no eye has seen, no ear has heard, no mind has conceived" (1 Corinthians 2:9). But here, questions still remain.

Already, But Not Yet

God's sovereignty includes His knowledge of the big picture, and He knows His purpose within that picture, only part of which He chooses to reveal to His people. That big picture looks something like this:

This Age	Age to Come
. . . Satan opposes redemptive work of God . . .	
Genesis 1–3	Revelation 20–21
1:1 First creation	21:1 New creation
2:17 Death	21:4 No more death
3:1 Satan disrupts God/man relationship	20:10 Satan forever out of picture
Ch. 3 The curse	22:3 No more curse
3:24 Access to the tree of life	22:14 Access to the tree restored
3:24 Cast out of God's presence	22:4 Forever in God's presence

Out of the Fall came sorrow, suffering, and death. But the bright part of the dark tragedy of Eden is that God intervened. As soon as man fell and suffering started, God announced the first prophecy of salvation for a world full of sinners lost and polluted by the first sin (Genesis 3:15). Through the seed of the first created woman, one was to come who would destroy the works of the devil and provide a perfect salvation. One man brought sin, one man would bring hope. The tree in the garden was the tool of sin, the tree at Calvary would be the tool of hope.

Many religions teach that a redeemer will come, but they don't see Jesus as that Messiah. To them, during the time between the Fall and the age to come, Satan will continue to run roughshod over the world. As a result, they believe that God's people will have to helplessly endure suffering and affliction until God establishes His future kingdom. This doctrine and many that followed, are part of what is called *eschatology,* meaning "the doctrine of last things."

> *With Jesus' life, the kingdom broke into history. The end broke into the middle. The one-day eschatological kingdom began its activity here on earth.*

But scholars such as British theologian C. H. Dodd took this theory further. Dodd described what he called *realized eschatology,* which simply means that with Jesus' life, the kingdom broke into history. The end broke into the middle. The one-day eschatological kingdom began its activity here on earth. As a result, everything that the prophets hoped for was realized, awaiting final consummation in the age to come. And the time line changed to look like this:

This Age	Midpoint	Age to Come
	Jesus	
	Satan defeated but not yet destroyed	

This change let the light of the future shine on the present, and we don't have to wait for it to come. Today we can enjoy part of our final victory in the everyday things of life.

And that's what we mean by the phrase "Already but not yet." The debt has been paid for redemption in the end, but Jesus' life folded part of that end into the middle so that God's people could enjoy not only eternal life, but abundant life here on earth as well.

Author Dallas Willard *(The Divine Conspiracy,* Harper SanFrancisco, 1998) says, "He slipped into our world through the backroads and outlying districts of one of the least important places on earth and has allowed his program for human history to unfurl ever so slowly through the centuries."

I like to look at the age to come as knowing I will be receiving a huge inheritance someday. Then suddenly, on an ordinary day facing ordinary things, someone comes to me unexpectedly and hands me ten thousand dollars as an advance on that inheritance. With that newfound wealth, I'm able to buy lots of things that would otherwise have remained out of my reach. Those dollars became a foretaste, a harbinger of what is to come when I receive the whole amount.

In Ephesians 1:14 we read about this early windfall as "a deposit guaranteeing our inheritance." I call it earnest money. "And you also were included in Christ when you heard the word of truth, the gospel of your salvation. Having believed, you were marked in him with a seal, the promised Holy Spirit, who is a deposit guaranteeing our inheritance until the redemption of those who are God's possession—to the praise of his glory" (Ephesians 1:13–14). First you heard, then you believed, then the Holy Spirit came to seal your relationship and become earnest money for your ultimate inheritance.

The focus of Jesus' message was the kingdom of heaven. Mark passed on Jesus' words as, "The kingdom of God is near" (1:15). Matthew wrote, "Jesus went throughout Galilee . . . preaching the good news of the kingdom" (4:23). Luke quotes the prophet Isaiah's words on the coming of the kingdom (4:21).

Instead of waiting until the end of the age to reveal His power and destroy satanic evil, Jesus declares that God has already acted to curb the power of Satan. At the end of the age, Satan will be destroyed. But for now, suffering still happens. Satan still walks about like a roaring lion seeking whom he can devour (1 Peter 5:8). That lion will not be ultimately destroyed until the age to come. But Jesus gave us power over him in the meantime.

> *At the end of the age, Satan will be destroyed. But for now, suffering still happens.*

The kingdom of God is at hand right now. Because of Jesus, we can bind Satan in the name of Jesus Christ. O. Cullmann interprets the binding of Satan as being "bound, but with a long rope" (as quoted by Dallas Willard, *Divine Conspiracy*) Satan is not powerless, but his power has been broken. He has fallen from his place of power, but his final destruction awaits the end of the age.

So Why Don't We Believe the "Good News"?

Jesus arranged for the delivery of His life to us and made it available to everyone. "'The time has come,' he [Jesus] said. 'The kingdom of God is near. Repent and believe the good news!'" (Mark 1:14). In his book *All for Jesus* published in 1854, F. W. Faber wrote, "Jesus belongs to us. He vouchsafes to put Himself at our disposal. He communicates to us everything of His which we are capable of receiving."

But many of us fail to receive what belongs to us. We fail to believe the good news. Why? Because the problem continues in that we have trouble seeing the kingdom of God as both future and present. God is *now* the sovereign King, but He must also *become* the sovereign King in the age to come. Because we have difficulty grasping this truth, we often live our lives as though we don't have the privilege of asking for God's protection and guidance. We put the ten thousand dollars of earnest money in a drawer and never use it.

In *The Divine Conspiracy,* Dallas Willard writes about what we can buy, instead, with the money:

> Jesus' enduring relevance is based on his historically proven ability to speak to, to heal, and to empower the individual human condition. He matters because of what he brought and what he still brings to ordinary human beings, living their ordinary lives and coping daily with their surroundings. He promises wholeness for their lives. In sharing our weaknesses, he gives us strength and imparts through his companionship a life that has the quality of eternity.

So where does that leave you and me? With power over Satan. All this is part of our early inheritance. Part of the kingdom of heaven. Before He left, Jesus said, "Anyone who has faith in me will do what I have been doing. He will do even greater things than these" (John 14:12). He also said, "I have given you authority to trample on snakes and scorpions and to overcome all the power of the enemy; nothing will harm you" (Luke 10:19). Willard writes:

> Every last one of us has a "kingdom" or a "queendom" or a government—a realm that is uniquely our own, where our choice determines what happens. . . . Our "kingdom" is simply the range of our effective will. Whatever we genuinely have the say over is in our kingdom. And our having the say over something is precisely what places it within our kingdom. In creating human beings, God made them to rule, to reign, to have dominion in a limited sphere.

But what did things look like before Jesus came? How did people endure suffering before they had received this part of their inheritance?

In chapter 1, we saw Job as he dared to change his perspective.

Remember, he lived before Jesus' time. He and others only hoped for the final inheritance with no thought there would ever be an early one. How did that play out through the deep trials he faced?

Bible

Slip up on the wheelbarrow, if you will, and look into the life of Job. The book in the Old Testament tells Job's story and bears his name. Its theme? The suffering of the godly and the sovereignty of God.

The story opens describing the protagonist, Job, who lived in the land of Uz, who was "blameless and upright; he feared God and shunned evil" (1:1). He was rich and described as "the greatest man among all the people of the East" (1:3).

Then we meet the antagonist. Satan challenges the piety of Job saying, "Does Job fear God for nothing?" (1:9). He challenges that if everything was taken away, Job would curse God. God said, "Very well, then, everything he has is in your hands, but on the man himself do not lay a finger." He gave Satan permission to try Job's faith by sending suffering his way.

One day four messengers came to Job with some very bad news. The first messenger informed Job that the Sabeans had taken all his animals and servants. A second messenger arrived and told how fire had fallen and killed his servants and seven thousand sheep. The third messenger described the raiding party that had stolen more of Job's servants and his three thousand camels. A fourth messenger told him all his children were dead. While Job's seven sons and three daughters feasted at the oldest brother's house, a wind had blown in from the desert and collapsed the roof on top of them.

Stripped suddenly of his wealth and his family, Job tore off his robe and shaved his head. But Job trusted God's sovereignty, so he offered his worship. "Naked I came from my mother's womb, and naked I will depart. The LORD gave and the LORD has taken away; may the name of the LORD be praised" (1:21). Job praised God instead of charging Him with wrongdoing.

God pointed out to Satan that Job had remained blameless and upright, feared God and shunned evil, and maintained his integrity—despite his severe trials (2:3).

But Satan persisted. "Bet he won't if you take his health," Satan said. So with God's permission, Satan afflicted Job with painful sores all over his body. And He who had sat at the city gate as a judge now sat outside the city with beggars, scraping his itching, running sores with a piece of broken pottery (2:7).

THE VOICES OF OTHER PEOPLE

Job's wife couldn't take any more. She urged Job to renounce his integrity, curse God, and die. Job explained to her that trouble as well as good comes from God. "In all this, Job did not sin in what he said" (2:10).

Then Job received a visit from three of his friends. They were so overwhelmed by Job's deplorable condition that they sat in silence and stared at each other for seven days. Eventually they talked. All three of them offered their opinions as to why bad things happen and what Job should do about it. Most of the book of Job describes these dialogues.

Eliphaz the Temanite based his answer on experience and said that Job suffered because of sin. He argued that those who sin are punished, and since Job was suffering, he must have sinned. Bildad the Shuhite suggested that Job was a hypocrite and that Job's trouble must be due to his sins. "If you are pure and upright, even now he will rouse himself on your behalf and restore you to your rightful place" (8:6). Jophar the Naamathite condemned Job for his presumption and sinfulness.

He concluded that Job was getting less than he deserved. "Know this: God has even forgotten some of your sin" (11:6).

All three men came to a similar conclusion: Suffering is the direct outcome of sin, and wickedness is always punished. They argued that one can see God's favor or disfavor by looking at a person's material prosperity or adversity. They wrongly assumed that people could comprehend the ways of God without taking into account the sovereignty of God, and that divine retribution and blessing may extend beyond this present life.

In his replies to his friends, Job maintained his innocence, stating that both the godly and ungodly suffer and both enjoy prosperity. He lamented his deplorable condition and tremendous losses, venting his anger at them for accusing him rather than bringing him comfort.

After these three friends finished offering their sage advice, a younger man named Elihu shared his slant on things. He said:

- God is greater than any human being, and as people, we have no right or authority to require an explanation of Him (33:12–13).
- Some things God does are humanly incomprehensible, but He will speak to us if we will listen (33:14–16).
- How we hear from God depends on the attitude of the sufferer. An attitude of humility allows God to intervene. Instead of learning from his suffering, Elihu accused Job of having the same attitude toward God as do the ungodly, which was why judgment still affected him (34:1–4).

- We should have faith in God Himself rather than demanding explanations, and that Job should change his attitude from one of entitlement to one of humility (36:22–33).

The Voice of God

When the four men had finished their explanations, God talked to Job out of a whirlwind, as recorded in chapter 38. God's response does not attempt to explain Job's sufferings, but by a series of interrogatories, He humbled Job. Those whirlwind answers addressed three conclusions regarding Job's suffering:

- Job was not meant to know the explanation of his sufferings. Some things about human suffering God cannot explain to us at the time without destroying the purpose they were designed to fulfill. We are also incapable of comprehending heavenly things with our human minds.
- God is involved in human affairs. Job and his grief meant enough to God to cause Him to speak.
- God's purpose was to bring Job to the end of his own self-righteousness, self-vindication, and self-wisdom, so he could find his all in God.

In the end, Job saw the sovereignty of God up close and personal. His wounds were still fresh, his children still dead, his riches still gone. But Job wrote, "My ears had heard of you but now my eyes have seen you" (Job 42:5). Job found a whole new relationship with God. And it was suffering that brought that kind of relationship.

Application

We learn about suffering at Job's expense, even though he lived before the kingdom of heaven had arrived.

God is sovereign. We cannot understand His workings by rational thinking alone. Faith must rest in God's love and our knowledge of Him. Sovereignty means that God is all-powerful. He knows all. He is everywhere present, and His decision is final (Jeremiah 10:10; Daniel 4:17). Therefore, once we've prayed every prayer we know regarding our circumstances and realize our power in Jesus' name, we wait for Him to answer in His way. That sometimes means He doesn't heal or bless in the way we would like to see it done, but sometimes it means He does. What we do know is that if we don't ask we never will get. "You do not have, because you do not ask God" (James 4:2).

Once we've prayed every prayer we know regarding our circumstances and realize our power in Jesus' name, we wait for Him to answer in His way. That sometimes means He doesn't heal or bless in the way we would like to see it done, but sometimes it means He does.

Suffering is not always a consequence of individual sin. We read in John 9:1–3, "As he went along, he saw a man blind from birth. His disciples asked him, 'Rabbi, who sinned, this man or his parents, that he was born blind?' 'Neither this man nor his parents sinned,' said Jesus, 'but this happened so that the work of God might be displayed in his life.'"

Three of Job's friends blamed his troubles on his own wrongdoing. Though some suffering is the consequence of wrong decisions, as Job discovered, much of it is not, although it is distantly related to the original sin (John 9:2–3; Job 1:1; Luke 13:4–5; 1:75–76). Whether we did something to deserve punishment or the pain was thrust on us for reasons outside of our control, God is the answer. Calvary made possible deliverance from sin, the root cause of suffering, but it didn't eliminate the kinds of suffering to which sin gave birth—until the age to come.

We understand ourselves and our lives in direct relationship to our understanding of the character and workings of God. When we realize that God's will toward us is good (John 10:10) and that He cares and communicates His caring to His children, as He did to Job, this changes everything. Faith must have a resting place. When deep suffering threatens the foundation of faith, as was the case with Job, an assault on our faith can destroy us unless we are firmly rooted in these truths. To do this while we're suffering, we must stay in the Word, in prayer, and in Christian fellowship with those who encourage us.

In times of tragedy we face the temptation of making God our adversary instead of our advocate. As Job did, we can focus on declaring our innocence and questioning the justice of God, or we can be sure we hold onto no sin, then bow in humility and wait for God to reveal Himself and His purposes to us.

The struggle of faith is a personal one. We each enter the crucible of life alone. We must test the mettle of our faith in God against uncontrollable forces and win our individual victories. There will be times when family and friends abandon us and we must stand alone. We should always measure their advice against the infallible Word of God and what He's speaking to our hearts.

Satan is everywhere looking for those he can hurt. "The LORD said to Satan, 'Where have you come from?' Satan answered the LORD, 'From roaming through the earth and going back and forth in it'"(1:7). It's important to remember that for now, Satan still hurts people.

You can sin in what you say. If you have a personal relationship with Jesus Christ and have accepted His gift of eternal life as well as abundant life, walk and talk confidently. Though Jesus hadn't yet brought the kingdom of heaven, Job realized that God was still in control. He had a larger perspective. He knew there was more than this, and so he admonished his wife to not talk like a foolish woman (2:10). You and I have the benefit of the kingdom of heaven Jesus brought. Shouldn't this be all the more reason—when things look bad and we're waiting for answers—to keep the faith and talk the faith.

Be honest with yourself and with God, and resist reducing the ways of God to a manageable formula that keeps life safe.

More important than reasons and explanations is relationship. God's purpose is hidden. He owes us no explanation. Be honest with yourself and with God, and resist reducing the ways of God to a manageable formula that keeps life safe (Isaiah 55:8). Sometimes He doesn't deliver in the way we think He should. Sometimes pain *is* a punishment for sin. But in all suffering, regardless of the source, we have access to God (Job 9:33; 1 Timothy 2:5). There are over three hundred questions in the book of Job. In the end, he didn't get reasons. Instead he got relationship and a revelation of God. He learned about suffering from the divine point of view. "My ears had heard of you but now my eyes have seen you" (Job 42:5).

Your attitude through suffering can make the difference. In his best-selling book *When Bad Things Happen to Good People,* Rabbi Kushner writes about Job: "Forced to choose between a good God who is not totally powerful, or a powerful God who is not totally good, the author of the Book of Job chooses to believe in God's goodness." Job still believed in God and maintained his spiritual integrity when things looked bleak. For all he knew, he'd never have a happy, healthy, prosperous day again in his life. He didn't know God would turn things around. "The LORD blessed the latter part of Job's life more than the first. He had fourteen thousand sheep, six thousand camels, a thousand yoke of oxen and a thousand donkeys. And he also had seven sons and three daughters" (Job 42:12–13).

At first Job served God because God served Job with material blessing and family and health. But until Job was left with nothing but God, he didn't know how strong his faith would be.

At first Job served God because God served Job with material blessing and family and health. But until Job was left with nothing but God, he didn't know how strong his faith would be. He had to lose it all. Then Satan questioned if God was worthy to be loved and obeyed if He didn't bless or protect from pain. Satan wondered if God could win the heart of man totally apart from His blessings. Job served God out of a heart of love regardless of what he got out of it.

One day I soaked in my bathtub as I prayed for my oldest daughter. I told God what I wanted Him to do for her, then I added, "You don't owe me this and I'll serve you no matter what. But please answer this prayer for my daughter." Job—and I—honestly presented our pain before the one we knew would hear. (13:3). Job didn't have the assurance of the kingdom of heaven that Jesus brought. You and I do. We know God is in it. We know the beginning and the end, as well as the middle.

Some things we'll never understand. As we have seen, God explains some things to us, but not all. Though Job got new kids, ten of them still lay in graves, and scars still covered Job's body. Sometimes after we find relationship with God and claim our ten thousand dollars as earnest money on our final inheritance, things will still happen that have no reason or explanation. Those are the times we just have to let God be God and trust in His sovereignty. (13:15; 19:25–27; 23:10)

Conclusion

I was born with a pulmonary defect, which weakened the muscles around my heart. As my condition worsened, my mother was told that I would die before I started school. She grieved. But one day, as a new Christian reading her Bible, Mom realized that this news was contrary to scriptures she'd memorized, such as, "And great will be your children's peace" (Isaiah 54:13). My mother decided to put her faith in God's promises, and she went out and bought my school clothes and enrolled me in kindergarten.

Mom's faith was tested often as I continued to miss many school days that year. At some point, however, things turned around and I grew stronger. Color returned to my cheeks. I started playing with the other children. By the end of first grade, I won a physical fitness award. And in the years to come, free from all heart problems, I became the biggest tomboy in my family.

My mom knew God was sovereign, and ultimately He controlled all things. Her faith in Him would have continued if I had died. But she realized that a foretaste of the ultimate key to "hell and of death" (Revelation 1:18 KJV) could be lived out right now. We could bind the not-yet-destroyed Satan on the suffering he had planned for our lives.

That realization changed the way my parents raised us. We "took authority over" Satan in all kinds of situations. My parents anointed us with oil for protection. They prayed for our illnesses. And I saw it work.

That realization changed the way I raised my children too. I "took authority over" Satan in all kinds of situations. I anointed my family with oil for protection. We prayed for our illnesses. And we saw those prayers work. Today, my children are starting to do the same, because we've accepted some of our inheritance for now.

Bible Study

Because God is sovereign, there is nothing that happens to you that does not first pass through His hands.

1. He works all things out for His ultimate purpose (Ephesians 1:11), both the good and the bad including:

- Good fortune

JAMES 1:17: "Every good and perfect gift is from ___________."

- Bad fortune

AMOS 3:6: "When __________________ comes to a city, has not the Lord caused it?"

- Life

JOHN 10:10: "I have come that they might have _________ and have it to the full."

- Death

1 SAMUEL 2:6: "The Lord brings death and makes __________."

Remind yourself of the things you're facing, over which God still maintains control.

____

____

2. *God is in control of this age.*
   - Human will

   PROVERBS 21:1: "The king's heart is in the ________ of the LORD; he directs it like a ______________________ wherever he pleases."

   PROVERBS 19:21: "Many are the plans in a man's heart, but it is the LORD's ______________ that prevails."

   - Wicked people

   PROVERBS 16:4: "The LORD works out everything for his own ends—even the wicked for a day of _______________."

   ACTS 4:28: "They did what your power and will had decided ____________________ should happen."

   - Satan

   LUKE 22:31: "Satan has asked to sift you as wheat. But I have prayed for you, . . . that your __________ may not fail."

   MATTHEW 8:31: "The demons ____________ Jesus."

• Nature

PSALM 147:15–17: "He sends his command to the earth. . . . He spreads the ________ like wool and scatters the frost like ashes. He hurls down his ________ like pebbles. Who can withstand his icy blast?"

PSALM 148:8: "Lightning and hail, snow and clouds, stormy winds that do his ______________."

• Illness

PSALM 103:2–3: "Praise the LORD, O my soul, and forget not all his benefits—who forgives all your sins and heals all your ________________."

MATTHEW 10:1: "He called his twelve disciples to him and gave them authority to drive out evil spirits and to heal every disease and ________________."

• Emotions

GALATIANS 5:22–23: "But the __________ of the Spirit is . . . joy, peace."

PSALM 30:11: "You turned my ______________ into ______________."

3. *God is in control of the age to come.*

God is also in control of the end of the story, when the coming of His Son will usher in the final kingdom of heaven.

• Destruction of the devil and his angels

MATTHEW 25:41: "Then he will say to those on his left, 'Depart from me, you who are ___________, into the eternal fire prepared for the __________ and his angels.'"

• Creation of a redeemed society free from evil

MATTHEW 13:40–43: "As the weeds are pulled up and burned in the fire, so it will be at the end of the age. The Son of Man will send out his angels, and they will weed out of his kingdom everything that causes sin and all who do evil. They will __________ them into the __________ _______________, where there will be weeping and gnashing of teeth. Then the righteous will shine like the sun in the kingdom of their Father."

• Perfection of fellowship with God

LUKE 13:29–30: "People will come from east and west and north and south, and will take their places at the __________ in the kingdom of God. Indeed there are those who are ________ who will be __________, and first who will be last."

• Elimination of all pain and suffering

REVELATION 1:17–18: "Do not be afraid. I am the __________ and the ________. I am the Living One; I was dead, and behold I am alive for ever and ever! And I hold the keys of death and Hades."

• Participation in eternal joy

JOHN 16:19–24: "Jesus saw that they wanted to ask him about this, so he said to them, 'Are you asking one another what I meant when I said, "In a little while you will see me no more, and then after a little while you will see me"? I tell you the truth, you will weep and mourn while the world rejoices. You will grieve, but your __________ will turn to ______. A woman giving birth to a child has pain because her time has come; but when her baby is born she forgets the anguish because of her joy that a child is born into the world. So with you: Now is your time of __________, but I will see you again and you will ______________, and no one will take away your joy. In that day you will no longer ask me anything. I tell you the truth, my Father will give you whatever you ask in my name. Until now you have not asked for anything in my name. Ask and you will receive, and your joy will be complete.'"

Dear God:

I'm so glad that You're the mastermind behind all that's going on in the world. Sometimes I get discouraged and wonder if there's a plan, then I remember that You are sovereign and that Your will prevails in all things. Thanks because those of us who are in You have ultimate eternal life to look forward to. But until then, You gave us a little piece of eternity through Your Son and the kingdom of heaven He offers. Help me understand what all that means as I live a life of victory. Meanwhile, help me always remember, "It is the glory of God to conceal a matter; to search out a matter is the glory of kings." In the name of Jesus Christ, amen.

Ah, if you knew what peace there is in an accepted sorrow!

—Madame Guyon

CHAPTER 3

The Process

We are the clay, you are the potter; we are all the work of your hand.

—ISAIAH 64:8

As I waited for the announcement to start loading our plane, I picked up a *Financial Times* newspaper lying nearby. On page three, an article by Gillian Tett entitled "Look Before You Leap" caught my eye. The article talked about Japan's punctual railway system, a symbol of the country's powerful economy.

But the busiest carrier in the world has become a symbol of another kind—a rising number of suicides. According to the article, throughout Japan, 1998–99 recorded thirty thousand suicides, 35 percent higher than in the early 1990s and double the level twenty years ago. With rising success comes rising adversity and rising pressure. As a result, a rising number of people who feel they can't take their struggles anymore have been throwing themselves under the trains. The article described the railway company's plans for discouraging further suicides.

They would place mirrors on the tracks and paint the railway crossings in dazzling colors to prevent would-be suicide victims from jumping. The article went on to say that, "The theory behind this is that if suicidal individuals are forced to look at their own reflections before jumping, they will be deterred."

Our Entitlement Mentality

Japan is not the only country where multitudes of people despair of life. Most industrialized countries—where conveniences and achievements abound—ignore personal depth and strive for a painless society. From the time we're born, we're protected from pain. As babies, we feel no discomfort that a clean diaper or powder or gentle shampoo won't fix. We learned our cries brought people immediately to our assistance, to comfort us when we fell down or feed us when we grew hungry. As we got older, we learned to reach for the Tums to soothe upset stomachs and Tylenol for headaches. We worked hard to be pain-free every day. Because of this attitude toward less-than-comfortable conditions, we have a particularly hard time facing struggles. We search for quick fixes for the immediate pain, without attention to its causes.

As a result, happiness and comfort become our goals in life. "As long as she's happy" becomes the mantra of the day. Comfort. Good food. Someone to love. Our fair share. Are these too much to ask for?

I have a friend who works in youth ministry. She had the opportunity to go to Calcutta, India, and join Mother Teresa for a couple of weeks at the House of the Dying, where men, women, boys, and girls wait to die. Mother Teresa described them as "Our treasures. They die without blaming anybody. Without cursing anybody."

My friend took pictures of the terminally ill patients there. When she returned, we sat together to look over her photographs. As I searched the faces of those who knew tomorrow would be no better than today—if, indeed, tomorrow came at all in their dismal, sick world—it struck me that I saw less despair on their faces than I saw on some I knew in our country when they couldn't find something good on TV. Both the perception of what pain actually was and how to deal properly with it were not only oceans, but worlds apart.

I wonder if these people live with less of an entitlement mentality and so are not surprised or overwhelmed when struggles happen. Of course, apart from a relationship with Jesus Christ, their eternities are not secure. But what of the time here and now?

Wanted: Deep People

I only knew real pain from a distance, until I was in my late twenties. I went on my own comfortable way and didn't wonder about God's justice. Then I encountered hurt for myself. My dad had an automobile accident in which he ruptured his spleen, and when doctors operated to repair the damage, they found pancreatic cancer. I tried to digest the tragic news that my dad would soon die, while keeping my home running and helping my extended family grapple and make the necessary decisions. But when I looked inside myself, I found little there. Nothing deep had been dug, because nothing of real significance had ever happened to me. I found a shallow person, one who didn't know what to do with the pain except to resist it.

Aristotle recognized this truth when he advised that no one should presume to teach ethics—what constitutes good—until after the age of fifty. He maintained that until one had sufficient years of experience, one simply does not have enough experience of suffering to teach others what is *truly* good and what is *apparently* good.

I once heard the story of a man who wrote a wonderful hymn about a tragedy in his life. He sat in church one morning and listened to a young woman sing his song. She had a beautiful voice by any standard. "Well, what did you think?" someone asked the man at the conclusion of the song. The writer remained silent for a few seconds, then answered, "She'll be really great when something happens to break her heart."

Working in ministry with women for more than a decade, I've seen that women's hearts can be broken in a variety of ways:

- Quiet or loud
- Deserved or undeserved
- Long-term or short-term
- Gradual or sudden
- Lone or shared
- Voluntary or involuntary
- Emotional or physical
- Natural or spiritual

I've also seen these women respond to pain in many ways, including:

- Playing the victim. *"Why is it always me?"*
- Giving up. *"I can't do it anymore."*
- Blaming God. *"How could You do this to me?"*
- Pretending the problems don't exist. *"Life is perfect. Couldn't be better."*
- Befriending the problems. *"I don't know what to do when things are going well."*
- Defining yourself by your pain. *"I am my pain."*
- Becoming bitter. *"I'll never trust again."*
- Leaning on difficulties. *"I can't move on. I've had it too bad."*

The list goes on. Though each response looks different, they have two things in common: They all resist the pain, and they all put self at the center of focus. C. S. Lewis appeared to do the same in *A Grief Observed,* when he described how God appeared to ignore his pleas: "But go to Him when your need is desperate, when all other help is vain, and what do you find? A door slammed in your face, and a sound of bolting and double bolting on the inside. After that, silence. You may as well turn away . . . What can this mean? Why is He so present a commander in our time of prosperity and so very absent help in time of trouble?" (Harper & Row, 1989)

There's Another Way

Lewis's words sound much like the responses we listed above. Resist the pain and focus on self. But then he sheds light on a better way to respond: "Aren't all these notes the senseless writhings of a man who won't accept the fact that there is nothing we can do with suffering except to suffer it? Who still thinks there is some device (if only he could find it) which will make pain not be pain. It doesn't really matter whether you grip the arms of the dentist's chair or let your hands lie in your lap. The drill drills on."

Lewis is telling us to lean into the pain rather than fight it. To forget entitlement and concentrating on self-comforts, and to yield instead to the lessons they teach. Aesop said it a different way:

> An Oak, which hung over the bank of a river, was blown down by a violent storm of wind, and as it was carried along by the stream, some of its boughs brushed against a Reed which grew near the sore. This struck the Oak with a thought of admiration, and he could not forbear asking the Reed how he came to stand so secure and unhurt, in a tempest which had been furious enough to tear up

> an Oak by the roots? "Why," says the Reed, "I secure myself by a conduct the reverse of yours: instead of being stubborn and stiff, and confiding in my strength, I yield and bend to the blast, and let it go over me, knowing how vain and fruitless it would be to resist." (*Favorite Fables,* retold by Amanda Atha, Bracken Books, 1987)

My friend Barbara said it like this when I talked with her recently about her plight of being married to a strong-willed, controlling unbeliever for the last twenty years:

> Through these years, I've learned to believe God's Word. When I need help, He's there. He renews my strength. Through prayer and worship, I feel like I've been on vacation and I'm ready to go again. If I hadn't known the Lord through twenty-three years of marriage, I don't know what would have happened. My only plan of action is just to keep standing.

C. S. Lewis and the Oak and Barbara—they all learned to lean into the troubles rather than resist them. They've learned the process. They've also learned to let go of their own comfort. Those who search the hardest for happiness can become the most miserable. But maturity brings with it a different idea of happiness, once we find a deeper understanding of sorrow. Those who have come by the hardest roads often discover that happiness should not be our goal, but it can be a by-product when we invest in worthwhile pursuits. Helen Keller once wrote in her journal, "[Happiness] is not attained through self-gratification, but

Happiness should not be our goal, but it can be a by-product when we invest in worthwhile pursuits.

through fidelity to a worthy purpose." (*Helen Keller's Journal,* Cedric Chivers, 1973). Richard J. Foster wrote in *Celebration of Discipline,* "The doctrine of instant satisfaction is a primary spiritual problem. The desperate need today is not for a greater number of intelligent people, or gifted people, but for deep people" (Harper & Row, 1978).

Barbara has become one of those deep people through the process:

> I have not known one day of peace outside the Lord. As I paint the picture of my everyday life, my spirit does not go along with the picture. My life sounds bleak, but I don't remember a day I didn't have a song in my heart. Even through the night. Even when things were being tested at home and pushed to the limit, I still felt the wonderful presence of our God. I know His arms are wrapped around me.

As your drill drills on, how do you learn to put your hands in your lap?

Bible

As a child, I spent many warm Ohio afternoons playing in the creek beside our house. I remember the chill of bubbling water as it moved around my bare feet and the gray clay from beneath layers of rock I squeezed between my fingers. As I worked the clay more, I rolled it between my palms. Beads of charcoal-colored water would run down my arm and drip from my elbow. Then I would gather my load of clay and take it to a nearby flat rock, where I carefully crafted dishes for my playhouse.

The process began by removing small stones from the lumps

of clay. I had learned that rocks left in the clay would crack my masterpieces once they dried. So I pounded, rolled, squeezed, and stomped on the clay to remove its impurities. Sometimes the clay would dry out too much while I worked, and I would have to wet it again with water from the creek.

Finally the prepared clay would be ready for molding. I pounded a round base for a bowl with my fist, then I wound snake-like pieces up the sides in a circular motion until they reached the right height. Next I would smooth out the holes, dents, and bubbles with more pressure and line up the dishes on another rock to dry in the sun. When I checked on them the following day, sometimes I would find a piece that had cracked around an undetected stone or weak wall. It had to be redone. Most, however, were ready to be painted. Only then was my work complete.

I'm reminded of these creek experiences when I read the book of Jeremiah. As a prophet from the priestly town of Anathoth, many scholars suggest that his name means, "Yahweh Throws." To a potter, throwing means "to form or shape on a potter's wheel." We read in Jeremiah 18:1–6, this reference to the process of making pottery:

> This is the word that came to Jeremiah from the LORD: "Go down to the potter's house, and there I will give you my message." So I went down to the potter's house, and I saw him working at the wheel. But the pot he was shaping from the clay was marred in his hands; so the potter formed it into another pot, shaping it as seemed best to him.
>
> Then the word of the LORD came to me: "O house of Israel, can I not do with you as this potter does?" declares the LORD. "Like clay in the hand of the potter, so are you in my hand, O house of Israel."

While reading these words, I could almost feel the cool gray clay again as I squeezed it in my hands. I went to the library and found books on pottery that gave me a deeper understanding of what this passage means to those of us who struggle.

The Process

To a potter, *throwing* actually means to make or create. The potter's business, as mine had been as a child, is to create things. He begins with worthless, decomposed granite that is filled with impurities and throws it onto his wheel. God chose the potter's house to communicate His message to Jeremiah. God also has something important to say to us in the dirty, undesirable workplaces of our lives where we're called to suffer.

The wheel mentioned in Jeremiah 18:3 is where the potter works on his raw materials. If the piece of clay the potter is crafting becomes spoiled, he stops the wheel and smashes it with his fist. The potter is not only good at creating, but also at re-creating: "But the pot he was shaping from the clay was marred in his hands; so the potter formed it into another pot, shaping it as seemed best to him" (v. 4).

Why is the potter so picky? Because each piece is unique and bears the potter's trademark—his own fingerprints. And if a dent or air bubble is allowed to remain, the piece will burst when it gets in the kiln. When a defect is found, the potter doesn't discard the lump of clay and start over with a new piece. Rather, he throws it back on the wheel, puts his hands firmly around it, and begins his work anew. He is adept at doing several things to remake the vessel:

Wedging. The potter kneads the clay, much like a baker works the dough. This activity removes all traces of air and foreign matter and is often done by cutting clay slabs in half and pounding them.

The clay then becomes soft and pliable and easy to work with. Nothing else can be done until this process is complete.

Centering. After the clay is ready, the potter throws it down hard in the dead center of the wheel. Both hands pull the clay to keep it at the center so it won't burst in the heat of the kiln.

Pressuring. The potter applies this squeezing maneuver in order to create the desired shape. When the clay dries out, he remoistens it by dipping his fingers in a nearby bowl of water and rewetting the clay.

Now the pot is ready to go into the furnace. Here, it receives a bisque, or first firing, and then is decorated. Finally it is glazed. This glazing seals, hardens, and waterproofs the pot. How valuable the pot will be depends on the temperature in the furnace. Earthenware, the least valuable, is made below temperatures of 2,000 degrees. Stoneware is better quality and is fired at temperatures above 2,300 degrees. Porcelain, the most valuable pottery, is created when the pot is subjected to the highest temperatures of all—above 2,670 degrees. The porcelain became valuable because it yielded to whatever it took in and through the process, and while doing so became a great pride to the potter.

Application

Leaning into the pain, forcing our hands to lie still in our laps, means yielding to the Potter's hands as He does this work in our lives, willingly climbing onto the Potter's wheel and submitting to the process of wedging, centering, and pressuring. Our ultimate goal is to become a vessel of the highest quality for the Master's use. So what will help us lean into our pain?

Solve what you can, manage what you must. You'll find some

Learn to do what you can do, and accept what you can't do, while learning to trust God through it all.

things you can do something about while you're in a struggling place. Other things happen to you, which you're powerless to change. Learn to do what you *can* do, and accept what you *can't* do, while learning to trust God through it all. You can't rule life's situations, but you can rule your heart. Reinhold Niebuhr, the leading American Protestant theologian of the '40s and '50s, once wrote a simple prayer on the back of an envelope: "God, grant me serenity to accept the things I cannot change, courage to change the things I can, and wisdom to know the difference." Whether it be a long-term illness, a difficult marriage, or financial struggles, solve what you can and manage what you must.

Face the struggle, embrace the pain. Be honest about what is hurting you. When we avoid the real issues and mask or sweep them under the carpet, the problems don't go away, they just transfer to other areas of our lives. Grieve in a healthy way. Get help from counselors if necessary. Your church can help you connect with one that's right for you.

Resist feelings of entitlement. If you don't feel the world owes you a living, you won't be disappointed when it doesn't give you one. Entitlement always brings about disappointment, because reality can never measure up to the images we create in our minds. Look up scriptures that deal with servanthood and dying to self. Volunteering at church or in the community will take you out of your comfort zone and into a servant position.

Seek contentment. When you desire to be somewhere else or someone else, discontentment follows. Contentment comes from many great and small acceptances (2 Corinthians 4:10), and it's an almost foreign concept to the world. You find it by feeding your mind and heart on those things that bring contentment rather than arouse desire—especially while you are going through a hard place. Elisabeth Elliot said that contentment comes when we find a new definition for our unhappiness. Paul wrote in Philippians 4:11: "I have learned to be content." Paul found contentment by leaning on God's grace for help when things were good or not so good, whether he was fed or hungry, had plenty or found himself in want. Contentment means equalizing your desires with your circumstances. Paul's arithmetic for contentment was to subtract his earthly wants so that something of greater value could be attained.

> *Contentment means equalizing your desires with your circumstances.*

Expect the trials. If you have an inadequate view of suffering, you'll have difficulty facing struggles, seeking instead ways to escape them and searching for easy solutions to immediate pain. By encountering some hell on this earth, we get a taste of what eternal damnation will be like. So trials could be our greatest mercy and the force that drives us to the foot of the cross. A dying patient makes peace with her Creator. A depressed mother turns to heaven for reinforcement. A disappointed student falls into the arms of God to find a faith of her own. God's plan for us in this life is to give us the benefit of heaven only gradually. By letting us struggle with the remnants of sinful nature and letting us know pain, we see the hell from which we were saved.

Learn compassion for others. Compassion means "with suffering" or "suffering with." Through compassion, we can learn more about life and gain more sensitivity and relationship with ourselves and others. Mother Teresa wrote that there is purpose to our suffering, because through it we can understand the suffering of the world. For Mother Teresa, compassion was essential to any work done in the name of Jesus. Compassion opens the hearts of persons to the pain of others and moves them to works of mercy.

Conclusion

In his book *Dark Threads* (Revel, 1979), Herbert Lockyer writes:

> Suffering, it would seem, puts either a window or a mirror in one's life. Some dear people meet suffering by taking out the window and substituting a mirror. In their trial and grief, they become introspective, morbid, and self-pitying. They see only their sorrow, their need, their pain, their urgency, their injustice. They have not learned to sing, "Go bury thy sorrow, the world hath its share."

The mirror Lockyer talks about could be the same one placed on the subway tracks in Japan, which reflects only self and the undesirable dirty potter's houses we find ourselves trapped within. It's the one that allows us to see only the vision of what's in front of us and not what God will make in us through the difficulties. Lockyer's window, on the other hand, allows us to see ourselves and others around us with new vision. By looking through a window rather than into a mirror, our experience of suffering can be made a blessing.

> *By looking through a window rather than into a mirror, our experience of suffering can be made a blessing.*

Flying home after speaking at a conference one weekend, I was forced to look through a window at work the Master Potter was doing in my life. The faces and tears of those I met were still fresh in my mind. I thought of the big problems each of them brought and about the words of wisdom God poured into me for them.

Could I have addressed that group of hurting people several years ago in my presqueezing, prepunching, premolding days? No. But God loved me enough to strengthen me for my own trials and to enable me to help others during theirs. Though I am far from finished, God has used the circumstances in my life to wedge, center, and pressure me into the person He designed me to be all along.

As the plane began its descent, I prayed quietly for the people I had met and for God's continued work in me. Then I remembered the words of an old hymn that just about said it all:

> Have Thine Own way, Lord,
> Have Thine Own way
> Thou art the Potter, I am the clay.
> Mold me and make me, after Thy will.
> While I am waiting, yielded and still.

All the while I'm praying, "God, get on with the process."

Bible Study

Toward the end of the Book of Jeremiah, the Israelites were taken into Babylonian captivity for seventy years. Big-time suffering. They didn't want to be there, but Jeremiah wrote a letter to the people, and they passed it around from tribe to tribe, since they couldn't watch it on TV or read it in a book. The content of that letter told them what to do—how to lean into, how to submit to the Potter—

while they waited through the process. Jeremiah's instructions in chapter 29 can still help us today:

1. *Get on with life.*

   v. 5: "Build houses and settle down; plant gardens and eat what they produce."

   How have you let life stop when you go through hard times?

   What can you do to jump-start life again?

2. *Help those around you get on with life.*

   v. 6: "Marry and have sons and daughters; find wives for your sons and give your daughters in marriage, so that they too may have sons and daughters. Increase in number there; do not decrease."

   How can you encourage those in your home, work, neighborhood, or church to get on with life, even in trying circumstances?

   What can you do better to convey hope through hard times?

3. *Forgive.*

   v. 7: "Seek the peace and prosperity of the city to which I have carried you into exile."

   How can you stop resisting your circumstances?

   Whom do you need to forgive? Self? Others? God?

4. *Seek proper counsel.*

   v. 8: "Do not let the prophets and diviners among you deceive you."

   How can you find more godly people to hang around with?

   What can you do to become the type of godly person others need to hang around with?

5. *Trust God to be faithful.*

VS. 10–11: "'When seventy years are completed for Babylon, I will come to you and fulfill my gracious promise to bring you back to this place. For I know the plans I have for you,' declares the LORD, 'plans to prosper you and not to harm you, plans to give you hope and a future.'"

How can you show God you trust Him today? Sing? Smile? Share?

What can you do to step out in faith, even before evidence of a happy resolution is forthcoming?

Dear God:

Thanks for the process that puts meaning in the madness of life. No matter what trials I face—quiet or loud, deserved or undeserved, long-term or short-term, gradual or sudden, lone or shared, voluntary or involuntary, emotional or physical, natural or spiritual—help me lean into and not resist the process through the pain. Help me respond the way You responded to hurt, disappointment, discomfort, and misunderstanding. Help me to go willingly to the potter's wheel for Your work in my life. We are the clay, You are the potter; we are all the work of Your hand. So let's get on with the process. Put me back on the wheel and do with me what You will. In Jesus' name, amen.

God creates everything out of nothing. And everything, which God is to use, he first reduces to nothing.

—SOREN KIERKEGAARD

CHAPTER 4

The Purpose

All things God works for the good of those who love him, who have been called according to his purpose.

—ROMANS 8:28

Connie put the finishing touches on the wrapped presents one Christmas Eve, when the outside wind-chill factor was sixty-three below. Her identical-twin fourteen-month-old daughters sat dressed and ready to leave for their grandparents' Christmas celebration.

The year had been a busy one for Connie as wife to the county surveyor, mother to infant twin girls, teacher of high-school English at a school some twenty-five miles away, and student working on her master's degree twenty-five miles in the other direction. She had finished her Christmas shopping earlier in the day, and Connie looked forward to a quiet evening with family.

But as Connie walked toward the kitchen to gather the presents stacked on the table, she saw smoke coming from the back of their turn-of-the-century Indiana farmhouse. Since no flames followed, she tried not to overreact and attributed it, instead, to the wind blowing smoke down through the chimney. Minutes later, however, smoke permeated the house and seeped from the wall near the living-room ceiling. Something was wrong.

Connie called her husband, who had already gone to his parents' house to help them prepare for the evening. Her mother-in-law answered. Before Connie could finish explaining what she'd seen, black smoke filled the rear of the house. "Call the fire department, quick!"

Connie and her fifteen-year-old sister, Anita, bundled up the twins and rushed them to the car, then Connie ran to the back of the house and opened the door to get their Labrador retriever, Rocky. By then, flames were shooting from the ceiling. Connie grabbed Rocky, jumped into the car, and drove to a neighbor's house, where she made another call to the fire department. By the time she returned, she remembered their Siamese cat, Ming, still in the house. Opening the door to their living room felt like crawling into an oven. When the heat hit her, Connie became disoriented and staggered backward. She stumbled outside, gasping for fresh air. Saving Ming would be impossible.

They waited helplessly in the car. Finally, Connie's husband came tearing down the gravel road followed by fire trucks. They fought hard, but nature's fury won. Biting winds had turned a small flue fire into a raging inferno that whipped through the house. Water froze in the hoses as the firefighters tried to stop the blaze. They couldn't go inside because the frigid temperatures caused their masks to freeze and obscured their vision.

"Why?" Connie asked in disbelief. She had trusted God's wisdom since she was a little girl. She remembered Romans 8:28, "All things God works for the good of those who love him, who have been called according to his purpose." That verse would later help her make sense of all that happened, but it was shrouded in questions that night, when by eight o'clock, everything they owned was gone—irrevocably, devastatingly gone.

The last thing Connie saw as she drove away was the porch

swing, where she had spent hours quieting the girls, burning and swaying in the wind. Neighbors and curiosity seekers lined the road to see their disaster, and Connie resented their intrusion into her mourning this private tragedy. They drove toward town in silence.

For the next seven months, the family lived in a mobile home. After the ground thawed, rebuilding began, and Connie tried not to look back. That July, the family moved into their new home with a promise of well-being.

Three summers later, however, their home was destroyed again. It started once more with a spark—an angry word, an unresolved conflict. It grew into an ember, ignored as nothing more than a couple's normal struggles, and not necessarily the makings of a big fire. Instead of seeking help immediately when smoke came, they assumed the problems would resolve themselves. But once the fire flamed, it began overtaking other areas of their lives, just as the first fire had swept through the old farmhouse. And an eight-year marriage was gone—irrevocably, devastatingly gone.

Curiosity seekers again watched and speculated, pointing fingers and intruding in this greatest tragedy Connie had ever experienced. Seven months passed between separation and the final divorce decree. But unlike the seven months after their first fire, when she had built and prepared for their family's future, Connie whined, cried, and wallowed in pity for herself and her babies. "God, I'm not seeing how all these things can work out for the good of those who love You and are called according to Your purpose. I just can't see it this time."

When Romans 8:28 Isn't Enough

Christians can know—though they may not fully understand and sense it experientially—that to those who love God, He works all things together unto good. The things themselves may not be good, such as Connie's fire and divorce, but God harmonizes them together for believers' ultimate good, because His goal is to bring them to perfection in His presence. Even adversities and afflictions contribute to that end. The active voice present tense of the Greek verb *synerge,* "He works together," emphasizes that this is a continuing activity of God. And His working is on behalf of "those who love Him," those who have been called according to His purpose.

> *God . . . works all things together unto good. The things themselves may not be good . . . but God harmonizes them together for believers' ultimate good, because His goal is to bring them to perfection in His presence.*

The word for "purpose" is *prothesis,* which simply means God's plan. God's Spirit directs each believer according to a definite divine plan—a map for our lives He drew beforehand, as described in Psalm 139:16: "All the days ordained for me were written in your book before one of them came to be." But as wonderful as these words are, you and I will never be at rest until we accept the truth that all things indeed happen according to a divine plan when we belong to Him. We first accept this truth by faith, which brings about our change in perspective. Then we can look at divine revelation since the beginning of time through those who've gone before, and see evidence of God's sovereignty and His process at work in their lives.

God has an eternal plan that includes all things, even the fall of Lucifer and the entrance of sin into the universe. Though Jesus died at an early age on the cross, His life continues and speaks more powerfully from eternity than if He had remained on earth. Why? Because of the kingdom of heaven He brought, the early payment, the earnest money He left you and me on our final inheritance.

That plan of God is centered in the glory of God, the glory of Christ, and the glory of the elect like you and me, whom He chose before the foundation of the world. In his book *Romans III* (Wm. B. Eerdmans, 1959), theologian Donald Grey Barnhouse writes:

> God the Father never had a thought apart from the Lord Jesus Christ and His glory. And then, here is the most amazing fact of all: the plan of God includes the glory of the elect, the glory of those who are called according to His purpose.
>
> Our lives are not the haphazard result of the moving of blind chance. All that comes to pass in our lives is according to the eternal plan of the all-wise, all-powerful and all-loving Father. When we understand this, we will never be moved by the accusation of some that we believe in fatalism. Fatalism comes from blind chance; but the divine plan comes from the mind and heart of the all-loving God. It is for this reason that we are well assured that everything helps to secure the good of those who love God, those whom He has called in fulfillment of His design.

Nothing can touch us until it has passed through the will of God, and everything that touches us will be used for His glory.

Nothing can touch us until it has passed through the will of God, and *everything* that touches us will be used for His glory. A definite purpose leading to a definite end. Barnhouse goes on to say:

> We may live in quiet assurance that all is well with us, even though we are passing through deep waters. . . . It would be wonderful if all things worked together for our good without our knowing it, and we would find out about it later. But is it

> possible, here and now, for us to know that all things work together for our good. To lay hold upon this fact is to calm the turbulence of life and to bring quiet and confidence into the whole of life. Nothing can touch me unless it passes through the will of God. God has a plan for my life. God is working according to a fixed, eternal purpose.

God uses our pain for His amazing purposes. He doesn't waste our tears. That His purpose be accomplished is of higher importance than our deliverance or immunity from suffering. He is not concerned with making us comfortable, but with teaching us to hate our sin. He sees something bigger than the trials we're called to endure. But He draws in close to those who need Him, as seen in these examples:

- Husband to grieving widow, Isaiah 54:5
- Comforter to barren woman, Isaiah 54:1
- Father to the orphan, Psalm 10:14
- Bridegroom to the single person, Isaiah 62:5
- Healer of the sick, Exodus 15:26
- Counselor to the depressed, Isaiah 9:6

Sharon knew this when I talked with her. While she lay in the hospital at one end of town after giving birth to their third son, her husband went into the hospital in another part of town for some routine tests. They found leukemia and he eventually died. Sharon said, "Sometimes God calms the storm, and sometimes He calms the child." Sharon had learned that God's purpose sometimes means delivering us from suffering, other times he calms us in the midst of the suffering. In *Knowledge of the Holy,* A.W. Tozer writes:

> God moves undisturbed and unhindered toward the fulfillment of these eternal purpose which He purposed in Christ Jesus before the world began. We do not know all that is included in those purposes, but enough has been disclosed to furnish us with a broad outline of things to come and to give us good hope and firm assurance of future well-being.
>
> We know that God will fulfill every promise made to the prophets: we know that sinners will some day be cleansed out of the earth; we know that a ransomed company will enter into the joy of God and that the righteous will shine forth in the kingdom of their Father; we know that God's perfections will yet receive universal acclamation, that all created intelligences will own Jesus Christ Lord to the glory of God the Father, that the present imperfect order will be done away, and a new heaven and a new earth be established forever. Toward all this, God is moving with infinite wisdom and perfect precision of action. No one can dissuade Him from His purposes: nothing can turn Him aside from His plans.
>
> In the meanwhile, things don't go smoothly. Within the broad field of God's sovereign, permissive will, the deadly conflict of good with evil continues with increasing fury. God will yet have His way in the whirlwind and the storm, but the storm and the whirlwind are here, and as responsible beings we must make our choice in the present moral situation.

Suffering forces us to stand naked before God, and it brings us to a place of greater trust in Him. We begin to understand the inside stuff about God. "The LORD confides in those who fear him" (Psalm 25:14). God sees evil and pain, and He steers it to serve His good purposes. The Bible tells us in 1 Peter 5:10 that suffering will "perfect, establish, strengthen and settle you" (NKJV).

It's all part of God's plan. Not Plan B or C. His plan, His purpose. And that plan calls for Christians to suffer. To encourage us, He writes some light moments into the scripts of our lives. Many Christians don't see God in their trials, thinking that if there are no miracles, God must not be at work. But God's plan is specific. Every detail is ordained from eternity past. It's custom-made for that believer by an eternal God.

BIBLE

As did Job and Jeremiah, David believed in the truth of God's divine purpose hundreds of years before the kingdom of heaven was "at hand" through Jesus.

We meet him first when the prophet Samuel, sent by the Lord to choose the next king of Israel, comes to Jesse's home in Bethlehem. Samuel had Jesse bring his eighth son, David, in from the shepherd's field to be anointed for the royal position. David's life would shortly go from the quiet of the bleating sheep to all kinds of suffering in pursuit of God's purpose for his life.

The first big challenge came when David faced Goliath. His dad had sent him to his brothers on the battlefront to take them grain, bread, and cheese (1 Samuel 17–18). David arrived to the ranting and raving of a nine-foot-nine-inch-tall Philistine giant, who challenged the Israelites to a showdown. None of the Israelites wanted to pick up Goliath's challenge as he stood ready to fight (1 Samuel 17:5–7), "they were dismayed, and greatly afraid" (1 Samuel 17:11 KJV). When no one else would speak up, David did. For this he faced harsh criticism. His brother said, "Why have you come down here? And with whom did you leave those few sheep in the desert? I know how conceited you are and how wicked your heart is; you came down only to watch the battle" (1 Samuel 17:28).

David's predecessor, King Saul, also criticized the young man's intent: "You are not able to go against this Philistine and fight him; you are only a boy, and he has been a fighting man from his youth" (1 Samuel 17:33).

Even Goliath himself mocked David as he stood before him. The Bible says, "he disdained him . . ." (1 Samuel 17:42 KJV).

But David's sense of God's purpose in the Valley of Elah overrode the opposition of these naysayers. It was this sense of God's purpose that caused him to see the monster and say not "he's too big," but "he's too big to miss." David knew Goliath's puny gods would never be a match for the great God David served. And we all know the rest of the story. David chose five smooth stones from the creek nearby, and he used one of them to kill the giant. And God's purpose prevailed, but difficult days still lay ahead for David.

It was this sense of God's purpose that caused him to see the monster and say not "he's too big," but "he's too big to miss."

Saul sent for David, gave him his daughter as a wife, and made a place for David in his kingdom. But soon the king grew jealous of David. Saul's son, Jonathan, became best friends with this new hero on the block, and the public began to praise him loudly: "Saul has slain his thousands, and David his tens of thousands" (1 Samuel 18:7).

Saul, the once-godly king who'd turned his back on righteous things, was about to get booted out of office by God. So he "eyed

David from that day forward" (1 Samuel 18:9 KJV). He set out to kill this young man who threatened to take over his throne.

During the twenty-one attempts on his life, David lost his job, home, family—everything he'd depended upon except God. Yet David still trusted in the sovereign purpose of the Almighty. During this time he wrote Psalm 54:

> Save me, O God, by your name;
>   vindicate me by your might.
> Hear my prayer, O God;
>   listen to the words of my mouth.
> Strangers are attacking me;
>   ruthless men seek my life—
>   men without regard for God.
> Surely God is my help;
>   the Lord is the one who sustains me.
> Let evil recoil on those who slander me;
>   in your faithfulness destroy them.
> I will sacrifice a freewill offering to you;
>   I will praise your name, O LORD,
>   for it is good.
> For he has delivered me from all my troubles,
>   and my eyes have looked in triumph on my foes.

God did triumph over David's foe, Saul, and David assumed the throne of Israel, as God's purpose dictated. David didn't know that many years later, One would come through his own bloodline who would bring a taste of eternity into the present. Still, David gave a hint of what would come. He knew that God's purpose would prevail, no matter what lay ahead. And he wrote:

They will tell of the glory of your kingdom
    and speak of your might,
so that all men may know of your mighty acts
    and the glorious splendor of your kingdom.
Your kingdom is an everlasting kingdom,
    and your dominion endures through all generations.
(Psalm 145:11–13)

Application

I can already hear your questions as you read these words and think of the times you've heard them from the pulpit. It's easy to see God's purpose in David's life from our vantage point. And with the benefit of hindsight, others, like Connie, can tell about the good that came from their losses. But you and I still have questions today about the things we face and the good that could possibly come as a result of those events.

Do things that happen as a result of others' sin work together for our good when we belong to Him? Yes, they do. Barnhouse says, "Evil from evil men can bring good to God's yielded people" (*Romans III*). Satan meant the death of Christ as his ultimate onslaught toward God. But God turned it into salvation from sin, and through that death, He took multitudes from the kingdom of Satan into the kingdom of heaven. God turned the fruit of sin's hatred and turned it into the plan of salvation, which showed His love to everyone and made it possible for us to have eternal life.

Are there exceptions to the plan or purpose of God for the believer? There is no limit and no exception to this promise. Barnhouse writes:

> The scale has been turned in our favor; all things are yours (1 Corinthians 3:21). And again, "All things are for your sakes" (2 Corinthians 4:15). And . . . all things are given to us in Christ . . . There are not exceptions to the sweeping breadth of this statement. And if all things work together for our good, then all the attributes of God, all the works of Christ and all the gifts and powers of the Holy Spirit are at work for our good.

Does God's purpose always involve suffering for the believer? It usually does, because we're sure to get the message that way. C. S. Lewis calls pain God's megaphone: "He whispers in our pleasures and shouts in our pain" (*The Problem of Praise,* MacMillan, 1962). Humans just get the message more clearly when pain is involved, because we don't want to repeat the process.

How do I know when to listen to people's rebuke and when not to? David faced ridicule from his brothers and King Saul and even Goliath. People will often say you're not qualified and that you'll never win against your giants. Others, like Job's friends, will blame you for what you're going through. Maintain people in your life for accountability, then always line up what they advise with what the Bible has to say.

How do I keep from looking at the size of the giant I face? David had found relationship with God during the good times. This sustained him through the bad. When you know God and all that He can do through His Word, you'll realize no giant can ever overtake you. The same truths apply to the big as well as the small obstacles you face.

How do I know God's will, and how do I keep from thwarting His purpose? The beauty of trusting in a sovereign God is that He sees all things. He knows what doors to open and which to close.

> *The beauty of trusting in a sovereign God is that He sees all things. He knows what doors to open and which to close.*

He knows where you'll come through and when you'll fail. But if you ask for His guidance each day, as well as strength for the battle, His purpose will prevail. Somewhere along the way, I stopped beating myself up for mistakes I make when I'm honestly trying to follow His leading. His grace is sufficient for you and me whether we've got a little or a lot, because like God told Samuel when He went to select David, "Man looks at the outward appearance, but the LORD looks at the heart" (1 Samuel 16:7).

Conclusion

After the divorce was complete and any hope of reconciliation gone, Connie began to find confidence and peace once again. She realized the true treasures—her life and the lives of her five-year-old daughters—had escaped this second fire, and they had to start again. After exhaustive searching, Connie found the perfect two-bedroom home in a different town. Old memories soon grew dimmer as they replaced them with new traditions and routines, and eventually a newer, bigger house.

The girls recently graduated from high school, where they were cheerleaders, participated on the tennis and swim teams, and sang in a Christian music group. As freshmen in college, they continue to serve God and come home frequently for visits in their newest house, complete with a cat, beautiful antiques, and a porch swing.

Connie still faces hardships, including a hysterectomy during this past year. But glimpses of God's work from the past make it easier to believe in His purpose. She admits that she's found a new depth in Him, not because of her pain, but because of her surrender of that pain to His plan. I think Frances J. Roberts sums it up best in her piece called "The Master Artist" *(Come Away My Beloved,* Kings, 1970):

> Thou seest but a part of the picture, but I see the design in its completion. Thou canst not know what is in My mind and what I am creating with the materials of thy life. . . .
>
> I make no idle strokes. What I do is never haphazard. I am never merely mixing colors out of casual curiosity. My every move is one of vital creativity, and every stroke is part of the whole.
>
> Never be dismayed by apparent incongruity. Never be alarmed by a sudden dash of color seemingly out of context. Say only to thy questioning heart, "It is the Infinite wielding of His brush; surely He doeth all things well."
>
> And in all that He does with a free hand, without interference, He can stand back and view the work and say, "It is good."

It is good for Connie and for you and for me—even when things still look bad.

Bible Study

Good things come from our suffering when we yield it to God. As I talk with women, these are some of the purposes of God they have seen become evident in their lives through their suffering:

- To develop dependence on God

2 Corinthians 12:9: "My grace is
____________________ for you, for my power is made

perfect in ________________. Therefore I will boast all the more gladly about my weaknesses, so that Christ's power may rest on me."

- To cultivate a mind like Christ's

PHILIPPIANS 2:1: "If you have any encouragement from being united with Christ, if any ______________ from his love, if any ____________________ with the Spirit, if any _____________________ and _____________________, then make my joy complete by being like-minded, having the same love, being one in spirit and purpose."

- To develop character

ROMANS 5:3–4: "Not only so, but we also rejoice in our sufferings, because we know that suffering produces _________________________; perseverance, ___________________; and character, ________."

- To learn obedience

HEBREWS 5:8: "Although he was a son, he learned __________________ from what he suffered."

- To develop self-control

PSALM 119:67: "Before I was afflicted I went ____________, but now I ________ your word."

- To understand the love of God

2 CORINTHIANS 8:9: "For you know the grace of our Lord Jesus Christ, that though he was ________, yet for your

sakes he became ________, so that you through his poverty might become rich."

- To understand discipline

HEBREWS 12:5–7: "My son, do not make light of the Lord's discipline, and do not lose heart when he ______________ you, because the Lord disciplines those he __________, and he punishes everyone he accepts as a ______. Endure hardship as discipline; God is treating you as sons."

- To understand wickedness

PSALM 37:14–15: "The wicked draw the sword and bend the bow to bring down the ________ and __________, to slay those whose ways are upright. But their swords will pierce their own hearts, and their bows will be ___________."

- To understand injustice

1 PETER 2:19: "For it is commendable if a man bears up under the pain of ____________ suffering because he is conscious of God."

- To teach us awareness of God's sustaining power

PSALM 68:19: "Praise be to the Lord, to God our Savior, who daily bears our ______________."

- To teach us humility

2 CORINTHIANS 12:7: "To keep me from becoming __________________ because of these surpassingly great

revelations, there was given me a thorn in my flesh, a messenger of Satan, to torment me."

- To develop knowledge

PSALM 119:71: "It was good for me to be ____________________ so that I might learn your ________________."

- To develop faith

JEREMIAH 29:11: "'For I know the plans I have for you,' declares the LORD, 'plans to prosper you and not to harm you, plans to give you _________ and a _____________.'"

- To develop thankfulness

1 THESSALONIANS 5:18: "Give thanks in all ______________________________."

- To develop perfection

HEBREWS 2:10: "In bringing many sons to glory, it was fitting that God, for whom and through whom everything exists, should make the author of their salvation ________________ through suffering."

- To teach us evangelism

2 TIMOTHY 4:5: "But you, keep your head in all ______________________, endure _________________, do the work of an evangelist, discharge all the duties of your ministry."

• To understand the struggle for the kingdom of God
2 THESSALONIANS 1:5: "All this is evidence that God's judgment is __________, and as a result you will be counted worthy of the kingdom of God, for which you are suffering."

Dear God:

Thank You because You work all things for the good of those who love You, who have been called according to Your purpose. Nothing can touch us until it has passed through Your hands, and everything that touches us will be used for Your glory. Help me to live life on purpose—Your purpose. I yield to that purpose. In the name of Jesus Christ, amen.

We do not first get all the answers and then live in light of our understanding. We must rather plunge into life—meeting what we have to meet and experiencing what we have to experience—and in the light of living try to understand. If insight comes at all, it will not be before, but only through and after experience.

—John Claypool, *Tracks of a Fellow Struggler*

CHAPTER 5

The Provision

No temptation has seized you except what is common to man. And God is faithful; he will not let you be tempted beyond what you can bear. But when you are tempted, he will also provide a way out so that you can stand up under it.

—1 Corinthians 10:13

Sherrie and her eight-year-old son, Brian, lived in Los Angeles in 1979. Money was scarce, so when Sherrie noticed unusual swelling in her legs and feet, she worked hard to scrape enough cash together to go to the doctor. He diagnosed arthritis and sent her back to work. But her condition grew worse, and during another trip to the doctor, Sherrie heard these words: "You have a fatal form of lupus caused by tissue degeneration. We give you only a few months to live."

Sherrie felt numb. Who would be mother for her son? Then she prayed, "God, please let me live to see Brian become an adult."

God heard her prayer and answered. To the doctor's amazement, Sherrie's health started improving from that day. While regaining her health, however, Sherrie went on temporary disability, which caused her to lose her job. That's when a further test came of God's provision.

Brian arrived home from school one day and found he and his mother had no more food. Seeing the cupboards totally empty, Sherrie remembered the words someone had told her: "Faith in God is action. Do what you can, and allow Him to do the rest." Sherrie got out the dishes and set the table.

"Mom," Brian said. "Why are you doing that?"

"Because we'll eat soon," Sherrie said.

Sherrie recalls the puzzled look on Brian's face, and Sherrie knew that her words sounded more certain than her heart felt. "What would you like for dinner tonight, son?" she said.

Brian remained quiet for a moment, then he said, "Chicken and rice."

Minutes later, they heard a knock at the door. Their landlord stood just outside. "Sherrie," she said, "I made too much dinner for my family tonight. Is it OK if I bring over the extra?"

Sherrie's throat tightened as she nodded and closed the door behind the woman. A few minutes later, the landlord returned with a warm dish. Sherrie and Brian lifted the cover to see four chicken breasts on a bed of rice. They ate and enjoyed that meal more than any they could remember.

"Brian," Sherrie said after the meal was finished. "I'm stuffed. But I could sure go for a big piece of chocolate cake and a cold glass of milk."

Immediately, they heard another knock at the door. The landlady stood there holding several pieces of chocolate cake. "I made this as well," she said. The woman turned to leave, then she looked back and said, "I'll be right back down with a pitcher of milk too."

Unbelievable As It May Sound . . .

God's provision. It makes no sense to the human mind. How could a great big God hear the hungry words of a woman and her child in L. A.? Or what about you? Think of a time God answered a prayer that only you and He knew about, a prayer that let you know that He knew and cared for you more than you could grasp.

We talked earlier in this book about ways to change your perspective. What about taking time to change the way you look at God's provision? Maybe you can't think of a time when God answered your prayer that directly. But peek in the window of Sherrie and Brian's apartment and imagine seeing that miraculous event take place. Then go back with me to Daniel 3 and the story of three Hebrew men who faced being thrown into a hot furnace for refusing to bow to the image of gold that king Nebuchadnezzar had made in honor of himself. The three men expressed their faith in God's provision when they said, "The God we serve is able to save us from [the fiery furnace]. . . . But even if he does not . . . we will not . . . worship the image of gold you have set up" (Daniel 3:17–18).

So King Nebuchadnezzar ordered the furnace be cranked up seven times hotter than normal and commanded that his strongest soldiers tie up the insurrectionists. The flames were so hot that they killed the soldiers who tossed the three men into the furnace. Then it was Nebuchadnezzar himself who climbed upon the wheelbarrow and changed his perspective. "Weren't there three men that we tied up and threw into the fire?" he said. "Look! I see four men walking around in the fire, unbound and unharmed, and the fourth looks like a son of the gods" (Daniel 3:24–25).

I've heard this story since I was a child, but it still gives me chills. Imagine the king ordering three men to certain death, only to find God Himself going into that furnace with them. Imagine the men, who loudly proclaimed their faith in God's provision and that their faith would not waiver whether they made it through the fire or not.

That three-Hebrew-children formula still works today. You and I show the faith, and God brings about the provision.

Finding the Faith, Accepting the Provision

About faith, Benjamin Franklin wrote in the mid 1700s, "The way to see by faith is to shut the eye of reason" *(Poor Richard's Almanack)*. Oliver Wendell Holmes also described faith in the mid 1800s, "Faith always implies the disbelief of a lesser fact in favor of a greater" *(The Professor at the Breakfast Table,* E. P. Dutton, 1931). Emily Dickinson wrote in her 1864 poem *No. 915,* "Faith—is the pierless bridge supporting what we see unto the scene that we do not." The writer of Hebrews wrote: "Now faith is being sure of what we hope for and certain of what we do not see" (Hebrews 11:1). And Hebrews 11:6 tells us that without faith it is impossible to please God.

We know that faith is important and that God has provided in the past for people like the three Hebrew children and Sherrie and Brian. Yet most of us have trouble believing when it comes to our own fiery furnaces or empty cupboards. Those are the times when we have more questions than answers, our emotions are dry and cold, and we succumb to natural thoughts such as, *I'll never get out of this one alive.*

> *There's something innate in us that works against faith.*

There's something innate in us that works against faith, even for the most knowledgeable theologian or powerful preacher. No matter what God says, our own thoughts will lead us to get the job done ourselves, or to say it can't be done, or to say that it's not God's will or that's not the way He works. We can always come up with something to counteract what God asks us to do.

And then there's the problem the other way. If we do find ways to trust God, do we do it to avoid pain? Does our motive become selfishness wearing a religious veneer? Or do we obey God because we love Him, regardless of how much pain we must endure?

In Exodus 20:21 we read, "The people remained at a distance, while Moses approached the thick darkness where God was." We can be like the people who resisted going into the dark places and failed to trust God to provide. Or, we can accept the things we cannot understand with patience. If we respond as Moses did, with full faith that God will be there in the darkness with us, at some point we will see God reveal His treasures. We shouldn't be afraid to enter into the clouds settling down on our lives or the fiery furnaces we're forced to endure. God is in it. His provision will be there—if we have faith. But what does that provision involve?

Bible

Provision is defined as a measure taken beforehand to deal with a need or contingency. We read a promise for provision from God in 1 Corinthians 10:13: "No temptation has seized you except what is common to man. And God is faithful; he will not let you be tempted beyond what you can bear. But when you are tempted, he will also provide a way out so that you can stand up under it."

> *Not* out *but* through. *That's what God's provision means. He doesn't promise to remove the hard places, but to go with us through them to safety.*

Not *out* but *through.* That's what God's provision means. He doesn't promise to remove the hard places, but to go with us through them to safety. God does not call anyone to anything for which He does not also equip them. And that provision has evidenced itself throughout Bible times in several important ways.

Provision No. 1: Lights and Complete Truth

God's provision for early Israel came through something called the Urim and Thummim. In Moses' time, the only person who could go directly to God in the holy of holies was the high priest. The people went to the high priest with problems, and the high priest went to God to receive answers through the Urim and Thummim. Though never specifically described, it means "lights and complete truth," and scholars believe that this provision was used by God to ascertain His will in various matters. This is how it worked.

God had instructed Moses to wash the priest with water and to put on him a coat, girdle, robe, and ephod, and a miter upon his head. Then in Leviticus 8:8, God told him to put a breastplate upon the high priest and in that breastplate to put the Urim and Thummim. Scholars think these may have been stones that the high priest cast to find answers for people who came to him with a crisis or major decision. He would "consult the Urim and Thummim," and the people would have their answers. Thus God "provided a way out so [the people could] stand up under [their struggles]."

In Matthew 1:17, we read, "There were fourteen generations in all from Abraham to David, fourteen from David to the exile to Babylon, and fourteen from the exile to the Christ."

The Urim and Thummim remained God's provision for His people throughout the first fourteen generations. We see men such as Moses and Joshua consulting God, which meant they sought the Urim and Thummim for answers. But this provision disappeared at about the time of David because the office of the high priest became so corrupt. God couldn't use them for this most holy job anymore. So was the provision gone as well? No way.

Provision No. 2: The Prophets

During the fourteen generations from David to the exile into Babylon, God used prophets to meet the needs of the people. It was generally a period of increase for the Israelites, and God's provision included prophets—those who spoke for God.

This prophetic provision played out in the life of one woman we read about in 2 Kings chapter 4. Elisha was the prophet, and an unnamed Shunammite woman was the person who benefited from God's provision. She and her husband had made a place for Elisha and his servant to stay on their frequent trips to Shunem. To repay them, Elisha prayed that God would provide a child for this barren couple. About a year later, God gave the man and woman a son, and the prophet watched the boy grow as he continued to visit the family over the years.

One morning, as the father stood with his reapers, the boy came running to him crying, "My head! My head!" (2 Kings 4:19).

A servant carried the boy in to his mother. She held him in her lap until noon. Then the boy died. The mother carried the boy up to the prophet's bed, shut the door to the room, and told her husband to saddle an ass for her. Her husband couldn't understand his wife's command with their son already dead. "It's all right," she said (2 Kings 4:23). Finally the husband realized there was no use in arguing with a woman, so he helped her prepare for her journey.

Soon, the woman arrived at Mount Carmel and found the prophet. Elisha sent his servant to find out if things were OK. "Everything is all right," she said (2 Kings 4:26). "Oh, and by the way, my son is dead. Could you come take care of him?"

Elisha and his servant followed the woman back to her home. Elisha stretched his body over the dead son, and the boy sneezed seven times and opened his eyes (2 Kings 4:35).

And indeed, everything was all right, just as the woman had said. She knew down in her "knower" that God's provision would carry her through this horrible situation.

Provision No. 3: Also the Prophets

During the fourteen generations between the exile in Babylon and the birth of Jesus Christ, Israel faced some trying times, including the seventy years in captivity we learned about in chapter 2. God raised up other prophets such as Jeremiah, whom we discussed in chapter 3, to come to God's people and give them direction. Unnamed people in nonspecified situations also realized God's provision, though times were really tough. Countless men and women benefited from all the prophets, reminded that God would go with them through everything—as long as they continued to trust in Him.

Provision No. 4: The Ultimate Light and Complete Truth

Then came the life, death, and resurrection of Jesus Christ, and God's provision took on a whole different meaning. One woman described in Luke 7:11–17 realized God's provision once again through the kingdom of heaven Jesus brought.

It was a small town in Galilee, near Shunem, the town where the prophet Elisha had raised a son back to life some nine hundred years before. Jesus approached the town gate of Nain one day, and He encountered a funeral procession carrying the body of a young boy out of the city. Jesus looked at the boy's mother, a widow, and his heart went out to her. He said, "Don't cry" (Luke 7:13).

Then Jesus did what the prophet had done hundreds of years before. He touched the dead boy and raised him back to life. Only now Jesus Himself was the provision, not the prophet. The people even said, "A great prophet has appeared among us. . . . God has come to help his people" (Luke 7:16). And the news of the provision of Christ spread throughout Judea and the surrounding country.

But then Jesus died. Did the provision die with Him? No. When Jesus was raised back to life, God's provision was elevated to a whole new level. We read in Matthew 27:50–51: "And when Jesus had cried out again in a loud voice, he gave up his spirit. At that moment the curtain of the Temple was torn in two from top to bottom." This curtain separated the holy place from the holy of holies in the temple. The fact that this occurred from top to bottom signified that God—not man—did the ripping of the thick curtain. God was showing that the way of access into His presence was now available for everyone, not simply the Old Testament high priest.

That means Jesus' life and death and resurrection brought the kingdom of God one step closer, handing direct access to God to each of us. We read in Hebrews 1:1–2: "In the past God spoke to our forefathers through the prophets at many times and in various ways, but in these last days he has spoken to us by his Son, whom he appointed heir of all things, and through whom he made the universe." No longer the high priest or the prophets only, but each of us now has a direct line to God through His Son, Jesus Christ.

God's provision started with the lights and complete truth of the Urim and Thummim, continued through the prophets, then came full circle through Jesus—the ultimate light and complete truth—to God the Father. That gives you and me carte blanche access to God's provision, no matter what we'll ever face.

APPLICATION

God's part is making the provision. Your part is accessing the provision through faith. So how can we, as children of God, muster the faith we need to get to His provision?

You have started the process already. By looking at God's track record, you've seen His consistent ability to provide for His people. I own an old tape by a gospel singer named Becky Fender, who sings a song with these words in the chorus:

> You can't believe what He is till you believe what He was.
> If you believe what Jesus did, you can believe what Jesus does.
> Don't you be downhearted, don't you fret, my friend.
> Jesus Christ, He did it once, I know He can do it again.
> ("I Give You Jesus")

Once you discover God's provision through His Word and the testimony of His people like Sherrie and Brian, start building your faith. You never know when you might need it to face a hardship and be able to know in a Shunammite sort of way, "Everything is all right."

Spend time with God in His Word and through prayer. The Shunammite woman spent time with the prophet, God's provision for her day. She knew him in the good times, so she was well aware of where to go when things got bad. She'd learned the routine—she had the problem, the prophet had God's answer. You can do the same by setting aside special times for you and God. He'll talk to you through Scripture and through ways He speaks to your heart. If you wait till crisis to pray, you won't know Him very well.

Get a heavenly perspective. The Shunammite woman didn't waste time listening to those who told her it wouldn't work. Sherrie didn't have the luxury of relying on anyone else but God. Our tendency when we face times of difficulty is to either cut ourselves off from others or talk to everyone else about our pain *before* we talk to God. Go to God first, and then to those with a heavenly perspective and a real handle on faith. Many of the right kind of people to lean on will be found through your involvement in a Christ-centered local church.

Remember God's sovereignty and your choice. God chooses, or allows, what we will go through in life. We choose how we'll go through it. The Shunammite woman proclaimed everything to be OK before she could see it with her eyes. Sherrie set the table before she saw any food. Build your faith and sing your song, whether the sun is shining or you face endless storms. God's doing His part; do yours too.

Build home and family on the foundation of Jesus. Jennifer joined me in my home one afternoon recently for counsel. She talked about some hardship her little boy, Devin, faced. "How do I prepare him for what lies ahead?" she asked. I gave her the idea to blindfold him in a room with all kinds of obstacles around him. Then I suggested she tell him to go forward only on command. That way, he would avoid a fall and learn to navigate his way to safety. My suggestion is the same for all parents: Prepare your kids to find their instruction from the ultimate Father through His Word and to go there for guidance in all parts of their journey.

Be ready for God to use you because of your experience through pain. For the rest of your life, you'll be qualified to help others. I made one of my many routine trips to the grocery store one November afternoon looking only for food, but I found ministry as well. Shelley cried at my cart, telling me this was her first Thanksgiving since facing devastating loss in her family. I understood. I'd been there, and I'd experienced God's provision through it all. I was able to wipe away my sister's tears and remind her of God's provision. I saw her just the other night at a basketball game, and I asked how things were going. She smiled with confidence and said, "We're doing great."

Conclusion

Twenty-two years have passed since Sherrie's miracle meal. I talked to her just the other day. She caught me up on Brian, now thirty years old, and his faith in God. As for Sherrie herself, she still faces hardship and money is still tight. God didn't deliver her out of all suffering, He's just continued to see her through every one of them. And Sherrie has learned to trust that provision. "Everything's all right," she told me.

It was true for the Shunammite woman, and it's true for Sherrie and you and me. "Jesus Christ, He did it once, I know He can do it again."

Bible Study

God's part is the provision, your part is the faith. Faith will change your life during the good days as well as the challenging ones. Amy Carmichael wrote:

> Blessed are they that have not seen, and yet have believed; and Blessed is he, whosoever shall not be offended in Me; even so, fully preciously He keepeth, fully preciously He leadeth, fully preciously He loveth even unto the end. *(Though the Mountains Shake,* Luizeaux Bros., 1946)

1. Take a closer look at faith and what it could mean to your life:

- To live by

GALATIANS 2:20: "I have been crucified with Christ and I no longer live, but Christ lives in me. The life I live in the body, I live by faith in the ______ of ______, who loved me and gave himself for me."

- To stand by

2 CORINTHIANS 1:24: "Not that we lord it over your faith, but we work with you for your ______, because it is by faith you stand ________."

- To walk by

2 CORINTHIANS 5:7: "We live by faith, not by __________."

- To overcome the world by

1 JOHN 5:4–5: "For everyone born of God overcomes the world. This is the victory that has overcome the world, even our faith. Who is it that overcomes the world? Only he who ________________ that __________ is the Son of God."

- To be delivered from the power of sin

1 PETER 1:9: "For you are receiving the ________ of your faith, the __________________ of your souls."

- To be supported by

PSALM 27:13: "I would have __________________ unless

I had believed that I would see the goodness of the LORD in the land of the living" (NASB).

• To be strong in

ROMANS 4:20–21: "Yet [Abraham] did not waver through ________________ regarding the promise of God, but was strengthened in his faith and gave glory to God, being fully __________________ that God had power to do what he had promised."

• To stand fast in

1 CORINTHIANS 16:13: "Be on your guard; stand ________ in the faith; be men of courage; be strong."

• To pray for an increase of

LUKE 17:5: "The apostles said to the Lord, '________________ our faith!'"

• To defeat the devil by

1 PETER 5:9: "Resist him, standing ________ in the faith, because you know that your brothers throughout the world are undergoing the same kind of sufferings."

• To overcome difficulties by

MATTHEW 17:20: "I tell you the truth, if you have faith as small as a mustard seed, you can say to this mountain, 'Move from here to there' and it will move. ______________ will be ____________________ for you."

MARK 9:23: "Everything is possible for him who ________________."

- To enter into the kingdom of God

ACTS 14:22: "Strengthening the disciples and encouraging them to remain ________ to the faith. 'We must go through many hardships to enter the kingdom of God.'"

2. *As a result of faith, you will experience:*

- Hope

ROMANS 5:2: "Through whom we have gained access by faith into this __________ in which we now stand. And we rejoice in the ________ of the glory of God."

- Joy

1 PETER 1:8: "Though you have not seen him, you love him; and even though you do not see him now, you ______________ in him and are filled with an inexpressible and glorious ______."

- Peace

ROMANS 15:13: "May the God of ________ fill you with all joy and __________ as you trust in him, so that you may overflow with hope by the power of the Holy Spirit."

Dear God:

No temptation will seize me except what is common to man. You are faithful and will not let me be tempted beyond what I can bear. And when I am tempted, You will also provide a way so that I can stand up under the trials. All this because of the provision You have made for Your people since the beginning of time. Thank You that I can come directly to You about everything that concerns me. And as long as I have faith, You will answer. Even so, Lord, help my unbelief. In the name of Jesus Christ, amen.

The world breaks everyone and afterwards
many are strong at the broken places.

—ERNEST HEMINGWAY, *A FAREWELL TO ARMS*

CHAPTER 6

The Progress

> But we also rejoice in our sufferings, because we know that suffering produces perseverance; perseverance, character; and character, hope. And hope does not disappoint us, because God has poured out his love into our hearts by the Holy Spirit, whom he has given us.
>
> —ROMANS 5:3–5

One morning I walked into the room with the overstuffed chair and picked up my Bible from the shelf. I settled into the chair to begin my time with God, thanked Him for all the things He had done for our family, and prayed for others. Then I filled my prayer with all the struggles I faced.

"God, I have prayed long and hard for these needs. Do You really hear me? Do You care what is happening to me? Aren't You going to do anything to help me?"

I finished my prayer, put my Bible back on the shelf, and went upstairs to awaken everyone for the new day. As I worked through the day, I thought about my small daughter Courtney. I wondered why she had started to wake in the night. There were no physical reasons, and I knew she felt secure. But her interruptions were beginning to take their toll on all of us. What was I going to do?

Soon I knew. I would just let her cry through the night and allow her to learn that Mom wouldn't come in every time she called out. Hopefully, this would teach her to sleep soundly till morning.

That night the opportunity came to try my strategy. My sleep was disturbed by Courtney's whimpers. I heard her stand in the bed and shake the sides for a response. I slipped out of bed and moved quietly to a hidden spot beside her door. I listened to her cry for much too long till she finally lay down and slept.

I was sleeping soundly when Courtney awoke with a second wail. I took my place again beside her door and watched from where she couldn't see until she fell back to sleep. Then I returned to my room.

A third time Courtney awoke. I felt perturbed and waited a moment to see if she'd quiet down on her own. But once again, she did not, and I moved toward her room to the hidden spot beside her door. After peeking to be sure she was safe, I slid to the floor and rested my head against the wall. Her cries continued as she seemed to say, "Do you really hear me? Do you care what is happening to me? Are you going to do anything to help me?"

Where have I heard these same questions before? I wondered. Then I knew. Earlier that day, in my prayer time, I had asked the same questions: "Do You really hear me? Do You care what is happening to me? Are You going to do anything to help me?" Courtney's cries changed to a whimper.

Could it be, I wondered, *that God had His own hidden place just outside my room, where He stands watching over me while I pray and cry to Him? Could it be He really does hear me cry but stands silent because I need to learn something—something that will make me grow stronger? Could it be—of course it could, that God does not bat an eye or move from that hidden place till I am once again safe in slumber of rest and release?*

I listened to the quiet of the sleeping child in the bed not far away. I sat longer in my spot on the floor and listened to the silent explanations from God. And I knew that when He appears to be deaf to my cries, He, too, stands in His hidden spot guarding me—and teaching me what I need to learn.

The Hidden Spot Remains

Courtney's nearly grown now, but the truth I discovered that night about my growth in hard places remains clear to this day. Along with Courtney, I have watched myself mature as a child of God through the things I've been through and have found fresh hope to go on. Though uninvited changes have occurred in my family's life, I have worked to keep as many things as possible constant and solid, while I allow the unalterable changes to challenge me into growth.

We discussed in chapter 4 how all things will work out for our good when we belong to Christ. A death, disease, or disappointment can actually propel us away from our love affair with comfort and into a new area where God longs to take us. What we perceive as bad may just be change. And without changes and the resultant stress, we'd make little progress, remaining unproductive, unmotivated, and uncreative. Stress can provide incentive for growth, but balance is a challenge, and it begins with the constants.

The Constants

Any time I talk with someone who has gone through a major life change, such as death, divorce, illness, or sudden tragedy, I advise them to keep as many things as constant as they can. Research has long reported that when people go through prolonged stress, serious illness can result. Much stress is triggered by change, and change, by its nature, is disruptive. It requires significant energy to adapt to physically, mentally, and emotionally. A major result of energy drain is increased susceptibility to disease.

Stress expert Hans Selye says it doesn't matter whether the stress involves good changes happening (eustress) or bad (distress), it takes the same toll, because the body doesn't know the difference (*Stress Without Distress,* J.B. Lippencott, 1974). So whether you've met the love of your life or lost him, found a new job or lost it, too much change can bring on too much stress, which can trigger a body breakdown. The energy we need to fight off infection is used up in the process of adapting to change. We need the constants to promote the growth.

The Growth

In my early years of teaching, I heard Dr. Glen Doman speak in a class I attended on the subject of growth. He remarked that some parents often say we don't want our children to grow up too fast—at least not before their Carters wear out. Then he reminded us that the parent of a special-needs child wants exactly that. "Time stands still only for the brain-injured child," he said.

Throughout the Bible, we're told to grow. Paul expressed frustration with those who didn't grow. "I gave you milk, not solid food, for you were not yet ready for it. Indeed, you are still not ready" (1 Corinthians 3:2). In Hebrews we read:

> Though by this time you ought to be teachers, you need someone to teach you the elementary truths of God's Word all over again. You need milk, not solid food! Anyone who lives on milk, being still an infant, is not acquainted with the teaching about righteousness. But solid food is for the mature, who by constant use have trained themselves to distinguish good from evil. (5:12–14)

Only death or severe retardation of normal growth causes time to stand still. You and I need to be growing. Just as my child matured in her bed that night, we're called to grow through the hard places we experience. I once heard about someone asking Michelangelo why he wasted so much marble while sculpting the David statue. He is said to have replied, "As the chips fall away, the image emerges." In his book *Hot Tub Religion,* Dr. J. I. Packer writes:

> God uses chronic pain and weakness, along with other afflictions, as his chisel for sculpting our lives. Felt weakness deepens dependence on Christ for strength each day. The weaker we feel, the harder we lean. And the harder we lean, the stronger we grow spiritually, even while our bodies waste away. To live with your "thorn" uncomplainingly—that is, sweet, patient, and free in heart to love and help others, even though every day you feel weak—is true sanctification. It is true healing for the spirit. It is a supreme victory of grace. The healing of our sinful person thus goes forward, even though the healing of your mortal body does not. And the healing of persons is the name of the game so far as God is concerned. (Tyndale House, 1993)

But hardship doesn't necessarily bring about growth. Struggles and growth aren't necessarily mutually inclusive. Sometimes, pain can keep you spinning where you are, or worse yet, send you backward. To discover what makes the difference, I find it helpful to take a look at the oyster.

This mollusk makes a special substance called nacre, which goes to work when an invading substance such as sand or a tiny parasite enters its shell. That intruder is coated with thin sheets of nacre. Gradually, successive circular layers are formed, until the foreign body is completely enclosed in the shell-like substance—a pearl.

Struggle and pain invade our lives with change and stress in much the same way as sand invades the oyster. Stress can be defined as anything that pushes us away from our equilibrium in any area—physically, emotionally, socially, or spiritually. All organisms on earth seek equilibrium, or sameness, and we resist change. Newton's law of inertia says that "a body at rest will remain at rest until acted upon by an outside force."

> *Struggles and growth aren't necessarily mutually inclusive. Sometimes, pain can keep you spinning where you are, or worse yet, send you backward.*

Well, it's those outside forces, those disruptive moments, as Gordon MacDonald calls them, those pains and struggles, those stresses and changes that we've been talking about throughout this book. The bad stuff is gonna come no matter what we do. Some people face a challenge and use it as a springboard to grow. Others allow misfortunes to define them and determine the course of the rest of their lives. In the same way, the pearl takes on a similar luster and color to that of the shell's lining. Only some of the pearl-forming mollusks produce the beautifully colored nacre that is essential for the valuable pearls. Others have dull shells, so their pearls never develop luster. As a result, they have become worthless.

God does His part by working on us from His hidden spot. But to become of value to the kingdom, we must grow. Mature as a Christian. This involves the process of conforming to the image of Jesus or as 1 John 3:2 tells us "to be like him." The process is never complete, but we are to keep striving. We read in Philippians 1:6 that God began the good work in us, and He is able to complete it by the time we finally reach heaven. But what kind of growth does it bring about in us?

Bible

We read the following scripture in Romans 5:3–5:

> Not only so, but we also rejoice in our sufferings, because we know that suffering produces perseverance; perseverance, character; and character, hope. And hope does not disappoint us, because God has poured out his love into our hearts by the Holy Spirit, whom he has given us.

Over and over, the Bible tells us to rejoice in our sufferings. The word *rejoice* in Greek is *kauchometha.* It means spiritual glorying in afflictions because of having come to know *(oida,* "to know by intuition or perception") that the end product of this chain reaction that begins with distress ends in hope. Then the fruit comes.

Perseverance

Perseverance means to keep going despite counterinfluences, opposition, or discouragement. Suffering brings about perseverance, from the Greek word *hypomonen,* meaning steadfastness or the ability to remain under difficulties without giving in. The King James Version renders it "patience." Only a believer who has faced distress can develop steadfastness.

During times when God appears to be silent, He isn't sleeping on the job. He's looking on from His hidden spot, getting us ready for the work He's called us to. But often, the hardest part of suffering is time. Quick pain is more easily endured. But when suffering goes on and on or demands the same monotonous routine, the heart loses strength and sinks into despair apart from God. But God is getting us ready for higher service and nobler blessings, and nothing can keep us from it when God's time has come.

Don't steal your future out of God's hands. Persevere. Give God time to speak to you and reveal His will. Psalm 37:7 tells us to "Be still before the LORD and wait patiently for him." "Let patience have her perfect work" (James 1:4 KJV). He knows your need better than you do, and His purpose in waiting is to bring more glory out of it all. Patience and perseverance takes away self-works. He desires that you believe (John 6:29).

Often, the hardest part of suffering is time. Quick pain is more easily endured.

Thomas Paine made a speech to American revolutionary troops facing a crisis of morale, challenging them to persevere:

> These are the times that try men's souls. The summer soldier and the sunshine patriot will, in this crisis, shrink from the service of their country; but he that stands it now, deserves the love and thanks of man and woman. Tyranny, like hell, is not easily conquered; yet we have this consolation with us, that the harder the conflict, the more glorious the triumph. What we obtain too cheap, we esteem too lightly: it is dearness only that gives every thing its value. Heaven knows how to put a proper price upon its goods; and it would be strange indeed if so celestial an article as FREEDOM should not be highly rated. . . .
>
> I love the man that can smile in trouble, that can gather strength from distress, and grow brave by reflection. 'Tis the business of little minds to shrink; but he whose heart is firm, and whole conscience approves his conduct, will pursue his principles unto death.

Paine's message? It's the same as Paul's: Keep on keeping on. The suffering will produce perseverance.

Character

Only a believer who has faced distress can develop steadfastness. That in turn develops character, from the word *dokimen,* which means "proof." The King James Version calls it *experience,* a metaphor taken from gold proved by purifying fire.

Adversity introduces a woman to herself and lets her know what is or is not inside her. "Character cannot be developed in ease and quiet. Only through experience of trial and suffering can the soul be strengthened, vision cleared, ambition inspired, and success achieved" (Helen Keller, *Helen Keller's Journal*).

Gordon MacDonald compares character to the part of the ship below the waterline. He tells a story of the man who built only on top of the water where everyone else could see. So when the ship wandered into the deep waters, it sank, because sufficient attention had not been paid below the surface where character grows. He goes on to say,

> Sub-waterline issues seem so unimportant when the seas are calm and the winds are favorable. So it's only when the storms hit and something catastrophic happens that we are likely to ask a different set of questions. Why wasn't the weight better distributed? What happened to that keel? When storms happen, we learn more about what's below the waterline of our existence than we could have learned in any other way. (*The Life God Blesses,* Thomas Nelson, 1994)

Joni Eareckson Tada admits her character didn't develop overnight. "My diving accident was not a puzzle I had to resolve fast," she said. "It was the beginning of a long, arduous process of becoming more like Christ. Somewhere after my first decade in a wheelchair, I started to see good things. The image of Christ slowly emerging" (*When God Weeps,* Zondervan, 1997).

Suffering is character made muscular, not for its own sake, but for God's. I am a more sensitive person, more effective in ministry because of sorrow and suffering. I have never spoken to a group who said no when I asked if they'd grown closer to God or stronger in character as a result of pain. Character is not about what happens to us but what happens *in* us. It's not about what others *think* I am, but about what God and I *know* I am.

Hope

I received a letter some time ago from Christine in New South Wales, Australia, which read:

> For the last three years, my family and I have been making our way through the pain of divorce. When I was at my lowest point, I went for a walk in my garden and felt sad that as friends mowed my lawn, they would mow down my little freesia flowers.
>
> But God let me know that no matter how the lawnmower or hail or anything else destroys the leaves of the freesia, the bulb is safe from harm, buried in the soil. It will only miss a season of blooming, and then it will be back.
>
> So, too, the most precious parts of my personality and my soul and spirit are kept safe in God's loving care—and after a season, I will bloom again.

Through her suffering, Christine has developed steadfastness, which has deepened her character, which has resulted in hope and confidence that God will see her through. And since Christine's hope is centered in God and His promises, she won't be disappointed.

Disappoint means "put to shame because of unfulfilled promises." God's love, so abundant in believers' hearts, encourages us in our hope. And this love is poured out by the Holy Spirit, whom He has given us. The Holy Spirit is the divine Agent who expresses to a believer the love of God. The reality of God's love in a believer's heart gives the assurance, even the guarantee, that the believer's hope in God and His promise of glory is not misplaced and will not fail.

Despair means we've lost hope. We look only at our own resources, find them lacking, and conclude that the future is hopeless. Few things are more important for mental health, more precious, than hope. Despair shows that preparing to handle serious troubles requires us to remove ourselves, our egos, from the center of love. As long as focus is on our own limited resources or our own collection of hurts and pain, we are blind to many larger issues.

The reality of God's love in a believer's heart gives the assurance, even the guarantee, that the believer's hope in God and His promise of glory is not misplaced and will not fail.

The human capacity to take whatever life dishes out and to come back is never to be underestimated. One of my favorite movies is *The Shawshank Redemption.* It is about a man named Andy Dufrane who was wrongfully sentenced to life in prison for killing his wife. Andy remained unfairly imprisoned for twenty years, enduring all kinds of injustices and watching others die out of despair. One day, after emerging from two weeks of solitary confinement for piping music to the inmates in the prison yard, his friends asked him how he had fared. Andy told them he'd had Mr. Mozart to keep him company. "They let you take your music?" another inmate asked.

"It's in here," Andy said as he pointed to his head. "That's the beauty of music. They can't take it away. We forget sometimes there are places in the world not made of stone. But there's something inside they can't get to, they can't touch. It's yours."

"What are you talking about?" his friend responds.

"Hope. Hope is a good thing. When you have hope, they can't drive a man insane."

By the end of the movie, Andy's best friend, Red, understood hope. "Hope is a good thing," he said. "Maybe the best of things, and no really good things die. Get busy living or get busy dying. . . . I hope to see my friend and shake his hand. I hope the Pacific is as blue as it is in my dreams. I hope."

Andy and Red and Christine exemplify the kind of hope the Bible tells us to have. And that hope will not disappoint us.

APPLICATION

The growth process reminds me of a Youth for Christ teaching model I saw once, which looks something like this:

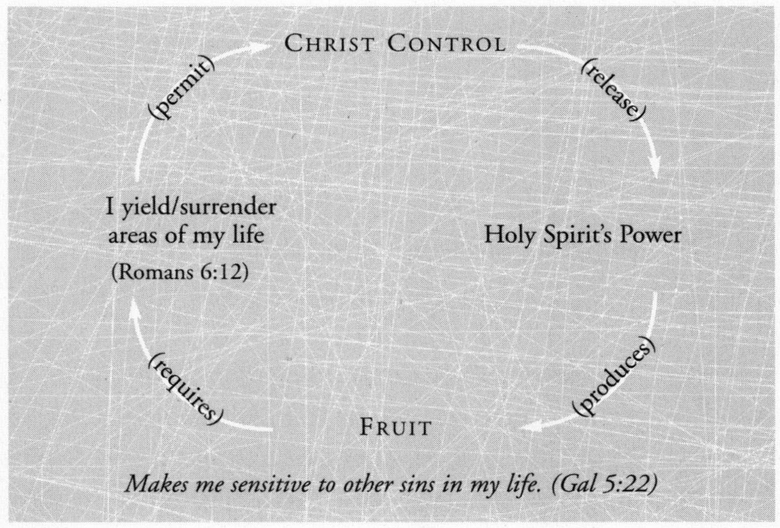

We yield or surrender our circumstances to God and permit Him to change us. Then as Christ takes control of us in those difficulties, we release ourselves to the power of the Holy Spirit. This produces fruit and requires that we surrender all over again. And the process never ends.

- *Yield.* To give up possession on claim or demand. To surrender or relinquish to the physical control of another.
- *Permit.* To make possible. To consent to.
- *Release.* To relieve from something that confines, burdens, or oppresses. To give up in favor of another.
- *Produce.* To give birth to or rise to. To give being, form, or shape to.
- *Require.* To claim or ask for by right and authority. To demand as necessary or essential.

Christ Control

"I give you my permission to __________."

"I release my hold on ____________."

"I yield/surrender __________ areas of my life."

Holy Spirit's Power

"I understand a continuous process of ____ is required."

"I desire that You produce ____ in me."

Fruit

"I yield, permit, release, produce, and understand what is required. Out of it I gain Christ's control and the Holy Spirit's power, and I grow the fruit."

Conclusion

We talked about the oyster and that the way it handles the irritants that come into its shell determines the pearl's value. The nautilus, or chambered nautilus, is a mollusk with a spiral shell, the interior of which is divided into a series of chambers filled with gas. As it grows, the animal moves forward into a newly formed chamber and builds a new wall that closes the chamber occupied last. He lives in the outermost chamber, but a tube passes through the little holes in each wall to the top of the shell.

Oliver Wendell Holmes wrote a poem he called "The Chambered Nautilus":

> Build thee more stately mansions oh my soul,
> As the swift seasons roll.
> Leave thy low vaulted past.
> Let each mansion nobler than the last.
> Till thou at length art free
> Leaving thine outgrown shell
> Beside life's unresting sea.

How about you? Are you making pearls out of your irritants? Are you allowing trying circumstances to propel you into growth? Go ahead. Leave your outgrown shell beside life's unresting sea.

Bible Study

Why the emphasis on growth? "If you have raced with men on foot and they have worn you out, how can you compete with horses? If you stumble in safe country, how will you manage in the thickets by the Jordan?" (Jeremiah 12:5). More on perseverance, character, and hope:

1. Perseverance

JAMES 1:2–4: "Consider it pure joy, my brothers, whenever you face trials of many kinds, because you know that the testing of your faith develops perseverance. Perseverance must finish its work so that you may be ____________ and ________________, not ______________ ________________."

1 THESSALONIANS 1:6–7: "You became imitators of us and of the Lord; in spite of severe suffering, you welcomed the message with the joy given by the ________ ____________. And so you became a __________ to all the believers in Macedonia and Achaia."

1 PETER 2:20–24: "But how is it to your credit if you receive a beating for doing wrong and endure it? But if you suffer for doing good and you ____________ it, this is commendable before God. To this you were called, because Christ suffered for you, leaving you an example, that you should follow in his steps. 'He committed no sin, and no deceit was found in his mouth.' When they hurled their insults at him, he did not retaliate; when he suffered, he made no threats. Instead, he entrusted himself to him who judges justly. He himself bore our sins in his body on the tree, so that we might die to sins and live for righteousness; by his wounds you have been healed."

1 PETER 5:10: "After you have suffered a little while, [God] will himself restore you and make you __________, ________ and __________________."

2. Character

ROMANS 8:29: "For those God foreknew, he also predestined to be conformed to the likeness of ______ ______, that he might be the firstborn among many brothers."

2 CORINTHIANS 3:18: "And we, who with unveiled faces all reflect the Lord's glory, are being ____________ into his likeness with ever-increasing __________, which comes from the Lord, who is the Spirit."

COLOSSIANS 1:28–29: "We proclaim him, admonishing and teaching everyone with all wisdom, so that we may present everyone ______________ in ___________. To this end I labor, struggling with all his energy, which so powerfully works in me."

PHILIPPIANS 3:12–14: "Not that I have already obtained all this, or have already been made perfect, but I press on to ________ ________ of that for which Christ Jesus took hold of me. Brothers, I do not consider myself yet to have taken hold of it. But one thing I do: Forgetting what is ____________ and straining toward what is __________, I press on toward the ________ to win the prize for which God has called me heavenward in Christ Jesus."

1 JOHN 3:2: "Dear friends, now we are children of God, and what we will be has not yet been made __________. But we know that when he appears, we shall be like him, for we shall see him as he is."

3. Hope

PSALM 25:3, 20–21: "No one whose hope is in you will ever be put to shame. . . . Guard my life and rescue me; let me not be put to __________, for I take refuge in you. May __________________ and ______________________ protect me, because my hope is in you."

PSALM 22:5: "They cried to you and were saved; in you they ______________ and were not disappointed."

ROMANS 9:33: "The one who ____________ in him will never be put to shame."

Dear God:

You tell us to rejoice in our sufferings, because we can know that suffering produces perseverance; perseverance, character; and character, hope. And hope does not disappoint us, because You have poured out Your love into our hearts by the Holy Spirit. Thanks for the hidden spot You occupy in my life to oversee all things. As You do that, help me to yield, permit, release, produce, and understand what is required for healthy Christian growth. Out of it I gain Your complete control and the Holy Spirit's power, while I grow the fruit in my life. Help me know what to keep constant and what to use to propel me into the more stately mansions where You long for me to live. Help me to grow and produce fruit through the irritants and disruptions in my life. In the name of Jesus Christ, amen.

Trouble and perplexity drive us to prayer,
and prayer driveth away trouble and perplexity.

—Melancthon

CHAPTER 7

The Prayer

The prayer of a righteous man is powerful and effective.

—James 5:16

When I was eighteen years old, my sister Anne, who was two years younger, and I went with our friend Laura, who was twelve years older, to a Bible college summer camp meeting in southern Arizona. We got jobs checking fellow campers into beds in an annex at the Bible college. The three of us managed a full twenty-four-hour shift and made extra money to spend on the way back to Ohio.

One night, following the evening service, I took a drive with David, the drummer for the services, who had become our friend. We went to a mountain overlook and surveyed the millions of stars above the lightning-bug-like objects below in the Arizona desert. Before I knew it, time had gotten away, and I asked David to get me back. I was more than an hour late for my midnight shift at the annex.

I grabbed my toiletries, gown, and robe from my dorm room, and made my way to the annex. As I leaned on the heavy annex door to slip inside, I noticed Laura sitting on the grass a few feet away. I decided she was mad at me for being late. So I hurriedly deposited my belongings and made my way out to Laura. "I'm sorry," I told her. "I'll make up this time tomorrow."

Laura looked at me and said, "I'm waiting for Cathryn and Stanley." Then she fell back into the grass. The sister and brother-in-law she'd mentioned lived in Indiana. Immediately I knew Laura had gone into a diabetic coma. She had warned us this might occur and had told us to grab something sweet to stick into her mouth if it did. Laura took 110 units of insulin three times per day, so I knew I should not waste any time.

I ran back to the dormitory and pounded on the door of the dorm mother. She awoke and told me to run to the infirmary to get a doctor and nurse. This was our only choice, as the Bible college was situated in the middle of the desert, twenty miles from a town either way.

I took the dorm mother to Laura, and I headed for the infirmary. After several attempts to get someone's attention, I discovered no doctor was on call that night. So I dragged the nurse and her medical bag out the door with me as I explained the problem. When we arrived at the spot on the grass, Laura was gone. I assumed the dorm mother had found some help carrying Laura to our dorm room. She was there.

I woke Anne and sent her to the annex to cover my duty. Then I assisted the nurse with medication for Laura. After a while, she pulled out of her coma and talked with the nurse. When things seemed to be OK, the nurse left. I turned off the light hoping Laura would sleep. Soon, however, she began hallucinating again, and she lapsed back into a coma. I ran for the dorm mother and nurse again, and we repeated the process a second and a third time.

Finally, at about four o'clock in the morning, Laura went into another coma. I started out the door, then I stopped and turned on the light. I walked to the right lower bunk bed where Laura lay, and I took her hand. She groaned and chattered. I prayed. I was out of other options.

God, if Mom and Dad were here, they'd know what to do. How to touch You. So would the other more mature Christians at this Bible college. But they're not. It's just me, and I need help. We're in trouble here. If You don't touch Laura, she could die. God please help us.

I turned off the light and climbed into the upper bunk of the opposite bed with my head toward the door. The burden didn't seem any less, I just knew I'd done all I could do. And I fell asleep.

Suddenly, I was wide awake. Facing the wall, I lay petrified that someone was in our room. I could only assume they'd come to steal any money we might have, and I didn't want them to know I was awake. Then Laura spoke. "Lynda, do you see that?"

I turned and looked into the middle of the room. I saw nothing, but Laura continued to talk. "That man. He's coming to you now." Nothing moved but my eyes. Then, like a vent pushing out warm air, I felt something come near me. I felt a hand lay on my right leg just above my knee. I could feel the fingers, but I could see nothing. Then Laura said, "He's coming to me now."

I felt the hand withdraw. A few moments later, Laura said, "He's leaving now." And I, too, felt something change in the room.

I jumped out of bed and ran for the dorm mother again. I didn't bother to explain this time as I dragged her with me. She walked into the room and said, "What happened? I feel goose bumps all over my legs."

Laura and I managed to get a couple of hours of sleep that night. The next morning, Laura took her insulin as usual, but she got sick as though she'd taken an overdose. So she reduced her dosage again the next time, and she felt similar symptoms. Laura cut down further, and by the next day, she didn't take any insulin at all. We finished our vacation with a well Laura. When we arrived home, Laura paid a visit to her doctor, who gave her a clean bill of heath. Laura no longer had diabetes.

From Angel's Hands

I went to college that fall and wrote about my experience in freshman English. I prayed a simple prayer that July 1970 night and received a miraculous answer. I can't tell you it was the words I prayed nor anything special I was doing with my life at that time. But I do know a miracle took place for someone who went to God when she found herself out of other options.

That was the biggest miracle I ever personally witnessed. Other times later on, I found myself in desperate times crying out to God again. My prayers were a bit more polished, and I felt greater faith based on my earlier experiences. But nothing seemed to happen. As a matter of fact, some twelve years after our miracle in the desert, Laura died of an unrelated illness. But she died free of diabetes.

Webster defines prayer as an address to God in word or thought. "Prayer is the link that connects us with God," A. B. Simpson wrote. "It is the bridge that spans every gulf and bears us over every abyss of danger or of need." And about the importance of prayer, John Calvin wrote, "If we consider how many dangers impend every moment, fear itself will teach us that no time ought to be without prayer."

My personal favorite image of prayer comes from Scripture:

> Another angel, who had a golden censer, came and stood at the altar. He was given much incense to offer, with the prayers of all the saints. . . . The smoke of the incense, together with the prayers of the saints, went up before God from the angel's hand. (Revelation 8:3–4)

I find it beyond comprehension that angels personally deliver our prayers to God—the smaller things as well as the larger, important ones. Once I left my favorite trench coat on an airplane after a flight. I was going through some difficult times, and I prayed that I would have the coat returned to me. "But," I added, "this isn't the most important thing going on in my life." Two weeks after the airline had given up ever finding the coat, I received a call to come and pick it up. I looked up at the Lord and smiled, realizing that this issue was important to God because I was important to Him. That answer to prayer gave me faith for some of the bigger things I still faced.

In this book so far, we've talked about suffering and the perspective, problem, process, purpose, provision, and progress that accompanies it. It is while on this journey through pain that we learn the most about the power of prayer. That's because we go to God most often when we hurt, feel most powerless, and find ourselves out of other options. A deeper relationship with God develops as a result, and we know how to pray in a more focused way, both for ourselves and others.

> When one who has not suffered draws near to one in pain there is rarely much power to help; there is not the understanding that leaves the suffering thing comforted, though perhaps not a word was spoken; and I have wondered if it can be the same in the sphere of prayer. Does pain accepted and endured give some quality that would otherwise be lacking in prayer? Does it create that sympathy which can lay itself alongside the need, feeling as through it were personal, so that it is possible to do just what the writer of Hebrews meant when he said, "Remember them that are in bonds, as bound with them; and them which suffer adversity, as being yourselves also in the body"? One thing we know, "God never wastes His chil-

dren's pain." (Amy Carmichael, as told by Elizabeth R. Skoglund in *Amma: The Life and Words of Amy Carmichael)*

God answers our prayers for deliverance from hard places, then He uses the experience from those hard places to develop relationship with us and make our prayers more powerful. How do we know this is true?

A Promise Is a Promise

We have God's Word on it. He tells us in Deuteronomy 7:9 that He keeps "his covenant of love to a thousand generations of those who love him and keep his commands." When my children were young, we had an understanding that whatever I told them would always be true, though sometimes what I promised them would come at a later time or in a different way than they had expected. If I promised that we'd go to the park and someone dropped by for a visit or an emergency arose, they knew the promise wasn't broken, it would just be delayed or would come in a different form. I can guarantee you that none of them lay awake wondering if I'd do what I said, but sometimes they did challenge me when they reminded me of my promise.

One day when Ashley was about four years old, she poured out the fish food on the bathroom carpet. I put her down for a nap and told her that she would lose a privilege that I had promised her. She looked at me, with brown curls framing her face and said, "But you already gave me that. You promised."

Because of my child's honest interaction with me, I realized as her mom that she was right. I had made a promise, and it was non-negotiable. So I sat on the side of her bed and said, "You're right. If you were the mom and I was the little girl, what would you administer as discipline for pouring out the fish food?" We agreed on a proper consequence, which would not break my promise. Why? Because a promise is a promise. And Ashley had my word on that.

F. B. Meyer wrote:

> There is hardly any position more utterly beautiful, strong, or safe than to put the finger upon some promise of the divine word, and claim it. There need be no anguish, or struggle, or wrestling; we simply present the check and ask for cash, produce the promise and claim its fulfillment; nor can there be any doubt as to the issue. It would give much interest to prayer, if we were more definite. It is far better to claim a few things specifically than a score vaguely. (*Streams in the Desert,* Zondervan, 1965)

But promises are true only if you know and trust them. Our faith releases the power of God's promises. "Humble yourselves, therefore, under God's mighty hand, that he may lift you up in due time. Cast all your anxiety on him because he cares for you" (1 Peter 5:6–7). You surrender yourself and the problem then trust Him to keep His Word and that turns the controls to God. One of my friends has a mentally disabled son named Adam. One day Adam went up in a small airplane with his dad, a new pilot. "Were you scared?" his mother asked once they had returned. "Oh, no," Adam said. "Dad was flying."

Prayer changes the course of history. Prayer moves the hand of God. Prayer is the key to the kingdom of God.

God wants us to have that Adam kind of faith. That happens when we pray. Prayer gets you alone with God. Prayer equips you for battle. Prayer changes the course of history. Prayer moves the hand of God. Prayer is the key to the kingdom of God.

God's Response

God gives us assurances in His word that we learn to trust as we get to know Him, but He still wants us to talk to Him about our concerns when we think He's been unfair or silent. David wrote in Psalm 35:17: "O Lord, how long will you look on? Rescue my life from their ravages, my precious life from these lions." And in Psalm 69:20, he wrote, "Scorn has broken my heart and has left me helpless; I looked for sympathy, but there was none, for comforters, but I found none."

Like David, we often question why God doesn't intervene. Some wonder if there is a God to intervene in the first place. Others wonder if God cares what goes on in our lives. Still others would have us believe that God doesn't possess the ability to intervene. But God's silence concerning our prayers occurs for at least four reasons:

Timing. We talked about God's sovereignty in chapter 2. He knows what He's doing, and when the precise moment comes to act, He will. But God uses His timing sometimes to fulfill His purpose, which we talked about in chapter 4: "Our God comes and will not be silent; a fire devours before him, and around him a tempest rages. He summons the heavens above, and the earth, that he may judge his people" (Psalm 50:3–4). God's timing also comes into play because of His desire that no one should be lost. I've questioned God before about why He doesn't just destroy those who do me and the rest of His people wrong. One day when I prayed this prayer, I found this verse: "Why do you hold back your hand, your right hand? Take it from the folds of your garment and destroy them! But you, O God, are my king from of old; you bring salvation upon the earth" (Psalm 74:11–12). God loves the sinner, too, so He gives them multiple chances to follow Him.

Faith. God tests our faith through His silence. We encounter one example of divine silence in Matthew 15:21–28. A Canaanite woman asked Jesus to heal her daughter from demon possession. But "Jesus did not answer a word" (v. 23). The woman kept asking—despite the disciples' opposition—and Jesus honored her faith. "'Woman, you have great faith! Your request is granted.' And her daughter was healed from that very hour" (16:28). Praying over and over again is like blasting through a mountain. You don't know if it will take one more or ten more blasts to make it through to the other side, it still looks just as dark as when you started. So what do you do? Keep blasting. Jesus called that faith.

Purpose. God has bigger things He wants to teach us, a bigger purpose He longs to bring about through a trial. We see this throughout the life of John the Baptist, Jesus' cousin. Because of their close family relationship, surely his mother Elizabeth prayed for her son every day: "Please, deliver John from the persecution he's under." Or "People aren't listening to him. Open their ears to hear what he's saying." Or "Deliver him from the prison." Or "Please, spare my son's life."

Yet through all the prayers she must have offered for her son's life, God's greater purpose prevailed—the kingdom of heaven. "After John was put in prison, Jesus went into Galilee, proclaiming the good news of God. 'The time has come,' he said. 'The kingdom of God is near. Repent and believe the good news!'" (Mark 1:14–15) John ultimately lost his life in this age, but God accomplished His purpose through John's suffering for the age to come. God may have bigger purposes for our suffering as well.

God tests our faith through His silence.

Motives. God sometimes doesn't answer because we don't ask for the right things. "When you ask, you do not receive, because you ask with wrong motives" (James 4:3). That's why it's important to learn how to pray, and we can learn how to do this by looking at earlier examples.

Bible

Many have attempted to teach others how to pray. One well-known formula involves four simple steps: A (adoration), C (confession), T (thanksgiving), and S (supplication). Let's look at four kings of Judah and plug in the formula to see things they did right and things they did wrong. All four of these kings encountered hardships, and that's what brought them to their knees.

Adoration

Adoration abounded during the bulk of Jehoshaphat's twenty-five years as king of Judah. He busied himself with building up Judah's defenses against Israel. So powerful was he, that surrounding nations left him in peace and even brought him tribute as a sign of his sovereignty over them. And he followed God: "The Lord was with Jehoshaphat because in his early years he walked in the ways his father David had followed. He did not consult the Baals but sought the God of his father and followed his commands" (2 Chronicles 17:3–4).

The king of Israel, Ahab, whose wife was Jezebel, so admired and feared Jehoshaphat that he sought to ally his kingdom with the kingdom of Judah. Jehoshaphat finally did go into battle alongside Israel and permitted his son to marry Ahab and Jezebel's daughter. The ensuing battle cost Ahab his life and Jehoshaphat a severe reprimand from a prophet for partnering himself with the ungodly (19:2).

The story picks up in 2 Chronicles 20, and it tells how the Moabites, Ammonites, and Meunites made war on Jehoshaphat. Immediately this king moved to his first strategy of war—he prayed. "Jehoshaphat resolved to inquire of the LORD. . . . The people of Judah came together to seek help from the LORD; indeed, they came from every town in Judah to seek him" (20:3–4).

Jehoshaphat stood in front of the people and adored his God. "You rule over all the kingdoms of the nations. Power and might are in your hand, and no one can withstand you" (20:6). He reminded God of his promise to deliver when they sought Him in the temple with true confession (20:7). Then he gave thanksgiving to God for His grace in giving them the land and temple (20:8). Finally, Jehoshaphat ended his prayer with these well-known words of supplication, asking God to help them in their immediate need: "We do not know what to do, but our eyes are upon you" (20:12).

And God answered. "Do not be afraid or discouraged because of this vast army. For the battle is not yours, but God's" (20:15). God gave them further instructions for how to overcome their struggle: "Take up your positions; stand firm and see the deliverance the LORD will give you" (20:17).

All the people of Judah and Jerusalem fell down and worship and adored God. Before they went into battle, Jehoshaphat reminded the people to have faith in God and they'd be upheld and to have faith in his prophets and they'd be successful. After he talked with the people, Jehoshaphat appointed men to sing praises to God on the front lines. When the songs began, God sent ambushes to destroy Judah's enemies. Jehoshaphat and his men returned "joyfully to Jerusalem" (20:27) and headed for the temple with their harps and lutes and trumpets to praise God again. The battle belonged to the Lord, but Judah accessed that power by praying and adoring their God.

Confession

Asa, Jehoshaphat's father had learned the importance of confession the hard way and the consequence of the lack of confession. He was assessed in Scripture as generally a good ruler, who destroyed pagan objects of worship and urged compliance with the covenant of the

Lord. He fortified Judah's defense posts and raised an army from Judah and Benjamin. The king of Egypt attacked Asa's army and failed because of Asa's faithfulness (2 Chronicles 14:2), whereas he had won over Judah's first king, Rehoboam, Asa's grandfather, because of his disobedience to God (12:1–4). Asa turned to God to help them in battle with the Egyptians, and God granted them victory.

Following the battle, we get a foreshadowing of what it means not to confess. A prophet came to Asa and cautioned him to remain true to God so he'd continue to enjoy God's blessings (15:1–7). Asa heeded the message by intensifying his destruction of idols (15:8), repairing the altar in the Lord's temple, and assembling the people to renew their covenant before God. And God brought them peace.

Asa seemed almost completely intent on following God's commands. But it almost proved his undoing. Though he'd eradicated foreign worship from Judah—including his own grandmother for making Asherah poles—he left some of the high places with pagan altars (15:17). This weakness, when allowed to continue without confession, ultimately caused his downfall.

During the thirty-sixth year of Asa's reign, the king of Israel built a fortress on the Israeli/Judean border. Asa panicked and made a treaty with the ungodly Arameans. Together they fought against Israel and took important cities. When Asa returned, another prophet faulted him for forgetting that it was the Lord and not soldiers who had given victory (16:17–9). "The consequence," the prophet said, would be war for the rest of Asa's days.

This time, Asa did not confess his sins. He got angry, in fact, and imprisoned the prophet while taking out his frustrations on the people. Later when Asa suffered a foot disease in his thirty-ninth year of rule, he refused to seek God's help, and turned only to the physicians. He died uneventfully a short time later.

Thanksgiving

King Uzziah exemplified thanksgiving in our prayers. In 2 Chronicles 26, we read how at the age of sixteen he became the king of Judah and reigned for fifty-two years. The Bible tells us, "He did what was right in the eyes of the LORD. . . . As long as he sought the LORD, God gave him success" (26:4–5).

And success he found. He warred against the Philistines and broke down the walls of three of their five great cities—one the town of giants and Goliath's hometown, another the center of worship for the fish god, Dagon. Uzziah also rebuilt other towns. God helped him against the Philistines and the Arabs. The Ammonites honored Uzziah's accomplishments with tributes as "his fame spread as far as the border of Egypt, because he had become very powerful" (26:8).

Uzziah's success continued. He built and fortified three towers in Jerusalem. He also built towers and dug cisterns in the desert to care for his many livestock. Uzziah employed large numbers of people, including a well-trained, well-equipped army. And "his fame spread far and wide, for he was greatly helped until he became powerful" (26:15).

But once Uzziah became powerful, his pride got in the way, and he turned from giving God credit to taking it for himself. When he did that, he became unfaithful to God, and he even burned incense to God, a sacrilege for which Azariah the priest and eighty other priests condemned him. Uzziah responded in rage, but the propriety of the priests' rebuke was immediately evident when Uzziah's forehead broke out with leprosy. This rendered the king ceremonially unclean, so that he had to leave the temple. Uzziah's leprosy got so bad that he had to be quarantined and he had to yield the reins of the government to his son for eleven years. Even in his death, Uzziah was so ostracized because of his disease that officials buried him *near* his ancestors, not with them.

Supplication

Uzziah's great-grandson Hezekiah became king of Judah following his father Ahaz and grandfather Jotham. The Bible's treatment in 2 Chronicles chapters 29–32 of Hezekiah's reign is fairly comprehensive. He is noted in 2 Kings 18:5 as one of Judah's greatest kings. He rebuilt and reconsecrated and reoffered and rerepented and led the people back to God. Even at his Passover festival, the people were so caught up in their devotion to and joy in the Lord, that they decided to extend it for another week. Hezekiah supported this at his own expense. We read in 2 Chronicles 31:21 that Hezekial sought his God and worked whole heartedly." Then we read of two prayers in his life that stick out in a particular way, one positive and one negative.

First, we read in chapter 32 that Hezekiah broke a treaty that had existed between his evil father, Ahaz, and the Assyrians. Because of internal rebellion, the king of Assyria was unable to retaliate against Hezekiah, but the king's successor, Sennacherib, did. Through his command, the Assyrians laid siege to various military towns and then moved on to Jerusalem (32:1–2). Before Sennacherib arrived in person, he sent an embassy from a town about thirty miles away, bearing terms of surrender for Hezekiah to accept (32:10–15). In Sennacherib's letter, he boasted Israel's impotent god would not be able to save His people from the Assyrians.

Hezekiah read the letter from Sennacherib, then he went up to the temple of the Lord and spread it out before Him. Then Hezekiah prayed to the Lord from adoration, "You alone are God over all the kingdoms of the earth" (2 Kings 19:15); then in supplication, "Now, O LORD our God, deliver us from his hand, so that all kingdoms on earth may know that you alone, O LORD, are God" (v. 19). And God sent an angel who destroyed the Assyrian host, forcing Sennacherib to retreat in humility (2 Chronicles 32:20–21).

The Assyrians lost 185,000 men (2 Kings 19:35), and Sennacherib returned home to two sons who murdered him. Hezekiah's prayer effectively defeated the enemy and brought honor to Judah's God and king from surrounding nations (2 Chronicles 32:22–23).

Hezekiah is known for another prayer, however. He had grown ill to the point of death. God sent Isaiah the prophet to tell him to get his house in order for his death. Hezekiah turned his face to the wall and prayed: "Remember, O LORD, how I have walked before you faithfully and with wholehearted devotion and have done what is good in your eyes" (2 Kings 20:3). Then Hezekiah wept bitterly.

God heard His servant's prayer, and He answered. He sent Isaiah back to tell Hezekiah he'd extended his life fifteen years. God did. But Hezekiah's life had already peaked, and his work for God had finished. Hezekiah prayed a prayer that God answered, but it was a prayer that didn't involve God's perfect will.

Application

God does not sit on the throne waiting to zap us when we do something incorrectly (Romans 8:1). But we can learn from the example of these four kings of ways to strengthen our prayer lives:

Finish strong. It's not the one who starts the race who wins but the one who finishes. Jehoshaphat, Asa, Uzziah, and Hezekiah did a lot of good for God as kings of Judah. Yet not one of them finished strong. Be careful in your walk with God over the long run. Don't fizzle out. In your prayers, adore, confess, thank, and give supplication. Be sure to cover all the bases so Satan won't enlarge a weakness in your life.

Seek daily direction. Through Ahab, Jehoshaphat allied himself with people he shouldn't have. He failed to listen to the counsel of the godly prophet who warned him repeatedly that this was a wrong move. We read in Proverbs 11:14, "For lack of guidance a nation falls, but many advisors make victory sure." This reminds us to surround ourselves every day with godly accountability.

Recognize and shore up your weaknesses. Asa removed most of the pagan gods, but he left ones in high places, which led to his country being at war for the rest of his life.

> *It's not the one who starts the race who wins but the one who finishes.*

Give God credit. Uzziah worked through many hardships. But when he got strong, he trusted his own and others' abilities instead of depending on God. He did no differently than the ungodly first king of Judah, Rehoboam: "After Rehoboam's position as king was established and he had become strong, he and all Israel with him abandoned the law of the LORD" (2 Chronicles 12:1). God is a jealous God. Whether it's good stuff or obvious sins, God won't play second fiddle to anything or anyone.

Pray always according to God's will. God had sent Isaiah to Hezekiah to tell him his time had come. He was a rich, powerful, godly king with all kinds of honor to his credit. But the last fifteen years added almost nothing to his success. Isaiah 39 tells how Hezekiah allowed the Babylonians to see all his riches. Isaiah prophesied that "Everything in your palace, and all that your fathers have stored up until this day, will be carried off to Babylon" (Isaiah 39:6). Without describing how or why, we read that God allowed this Babylonian takeover "to test him [Hezekiah] and to know everything that was in his heart" (2 Chronicles 32:31).

Then we read in the 2 Chronicles 32:25–26 a description of Hezekiah following his healing and life extension: "But Hezekiah's heart was proud and he did not respond to the kindness shown him; therefore the LORD's wrath was on him and on Judah and Jerusalem."

My dad used to teach about God's will—His *perfect* will, His *permissive* will, and His *acceptable* will. We say we want God's perfect will, but we often settle for His acceptable will, or for no will at all. You and I can't see what lies ahead or the purpose that God has for accomplishing a certain end. It is possible, like Hezekiah, to move God through prayer and trade His perfect will for His permissive or acceptable will. We pray for the better instead of the best. Never, never pray without first praying that God's will be done.

Conclusion

I wonder what things looked like from God's throne today. Was He sad because the angels had no prayer from you to deliver to Him? Was He happy that you looked to Him to get you out of a fix? Was He pleased with your growth in faith? Was He encouraged as you asked for wisdom?

Prayer is our connection to God. Use it wisely, but use it.

Bible Study

Prayer puts us in touch with God, and His power becomes available to us as we struggle with life. It has been said that we don't come to the throne to make demands or to get man's will done in heaven. We come to get God's will done on earth (Luke 22:42). As a result, outward discipline becomes inward character in you and me.

1. Memorize these promises of who God will be for you through your struggles:

- Refuge

PSALM 46:1: "God is our ____________ and ________________, an ever-present help in trouble."

- Shield

PSALM 3:2–3: "Many are saying of me, 'God will not deliver him.' But you are a ____________ around me, O LORD; you bestow glory on me and lift up my ________."

- Strength

PSALM 28:7: "The LORD is my strength and my shield; my heart trust in him, and I am ____________."

- Shepherd

PSALM 23:1: "The LORD is my shepherd, I shall not be in ________."

- Comfort

2 CORINTHIANS 1:3–4: "Praise be to the God and Father of our Lord Jesus Christ . . . who ________________ us in all our ________________, so that we can comfort those in any trouble with the comfort we ourselves have received from God."

- Provision

EPHESIANS 3:20–21: "Now to him who is able to do immeasurably more than all we ______ or ______________, according to his power that is at work within us, to him be glory."

- Available

JAMES 4:8: "Come near to God and he will ________ ________ to you."

- Supplier

PHILIPPIANS 4:19: "And my God will meet all your needs according to his ________________ ____________ in Christ Jesus."

- Sufficient

2 CORINTHIANS 12:9–10: "But he said to me, 'My grace is ____________________ for you, for my power is made perfect in weakness.' Therefore I will boast all the more gladly about my ____________________, so that Christ's power may rest on me. That is why, for Christ's sake, I delight in weaknesses, in insults, in hardships, in persecutions, in difficulties. For when I am ________, then I am ____________."

2. *Memorize these scriptures on prayer and its importance:*

MATTHEW 18:19–20: "If two of you on earth agree about anything you ask for, it will be ________ for you by my Father in heaven. For where two or three ________ ________________ in my name, there am I with them."

JOHN 15:16: "The Father will give you whatever you ask ____ ____ ________."

JOHN 15:7: "If you remain in me and my words [the Bible] remain in you, ask ________________ ______ ________, and it will be given you."

3. Review the five steps Jesus gave the disciples in Luke 11 (KJV), for how to pray. What do they mean to you?

- "Our Father which art in heaven, Hallowed be thy name" (v. 2).

- "Thy kingdom come. Thy will be done, as in heaven, so in earth" (v. 2).

- "Give us day by day our daily bread" (v. 3).

- "And forgive us our sins; for we also forgive every one that is indebted to us" (v. 4).

- "And lead us not into temptation; but deliver us from evil" (v. 4).

Dear God:

You are holy and good and righteous and sovereign. Forgive me for doubting You. Thank You for all the prayers You've answered in the past. Now, Lord, You know what I face today. Help me trust in Your promises, grow in my faith, wait on Your timing, and finish strong. Most of all, help me always remember that the prayer of a righteous man or woman is powerful and effective. In the name of Jesus Christ, amen.

Wise Man: One who sees the storm coming before the clouds appear.

—Elbert Hubbard

If you want peace, be prepared for war.

—Author unknown

CHAPTER *8*

The Preparation

As long as it is day, we must do the work of him who sent me.

Night is coming, when no one can work.

—JOHN 9:4

Focus on the Family hired me to become editor of their new magazine during the spring break of the university where I taught in Ohio. After accepting the job, I had a half semester to finish teaching, a house to sell in Ohio, a house to buy in Colorado, three children to prepare to leave, and the magazine's first issue to begin. The man who hired me, Dean Merrill, asked me which writers I'd like to have in the first issue. I named some of my favorites. Then I stopped and said, "But I don't want to put all the best ones in one issue. Who will write for the subsequent ones?"

Dean's reply came across the phone. "Write every issue as though it was your last. When you need more, it'll be there."

Dean was right. I plunged headfirst into the magazine, and for the six years I served as editor, we were never without quality writers. The larger truth involved, however, has spilled over into other areas of my life.

Because we know pain is going to happen, we sometimes live in fear of what lies ahead. Fear can also cause us to live between two dreads, a distinctly remembered tribulation and the fear of its return. Fear can paralyze us and keep us from living productive lives. But as we discussed earlier, God not only promises us eternal life; He promises us abundant life too.

So how do we keep fear from paralyzing us? What's the key to being prepared for what lies ahead?

Wise Worry

As a child, I often heard my pastor dad say, "If God's people would draw near to Him on the mountaintops, when they got into the valley, they'd find Him really close." We've been reminded of this truth throughout this book.

I call this living for the best and preparing for the worst. Consider the following Aesop fable:

> A commonwealth of Ants, having, after a busy summer, provided everything for their wants in the winter, were about shutting themselves up for that dreary season, when a Grasshopper in great distress, and in dread of perishing with cold and hunger, approached their avenues, and with great humility begged they would relieve his wants, and permit him to take shelter in any corner of their comfortable mansion. One of the Ants asked him how he had disposed of his time in summer, had he not taken pains and laid in a stock, as they had done? Alas! My friends, says he, I passed away the time merrily and pleasantly, in drinking, singing, and dancing, and never once thought of winter. If that be the case, replied the Ant, all I have to say is this: that they who drink, sing, and dance in the summer, run a great risk of starving in the winter. (*Favorite Fables*)

The ant in this story knew how to live for the best while she prepared for the worst. After all, she knew winter was coming, unlike the grasshopper who lived as though he'd always encounter sunshine and warm days. But it was the preparations of the ant that sustained her in the cold months that followed. The Bible even talks about it:

> Go to the ant, you sluggard;
> consider its ways and be wise!
> It has no commander,
> no overseer or ruler,
> yet it stores its provisions in summer
> and gathers its food at harvest.
> How long will you lie there, you sluggard?
> When will you get up from your sleep?
> A little sleep, a little slumber,
> a little folding of the hands to rest—
> and poverty will come on you like a bandit
> and scarcity like an armed man.
> (Proverbs 6:6–11)

I remember helping my mom can vegetables in the summer for the cold Ohio days that would follow. While you and I can't directly "can up" for tragedy or suffering, we can do a lot to be prepared. Because of its unpredictable nature, pain causes us to search our inner resources for ways to respond. Suffering always challenges our faith in God's ever-present love and often reminds us to reach out to others for comfort.

As we experience hard places, we can discover gifts of strength and courage and trust in God that we learned through a deliberate effort in the more comfortable times. These gifts may never have been discovered had not the suffering emerged. And the source of the strength we need to endure the trials can largely be found before we ever enter the valley or winter of our lives.

But it's not easy work. You're busy preparing while others are playing. Living for the best while preparing for the worst also involves a delicate balance between wisdom and fear.

When my Ashley was in elementary school, she got really fearful at night and usually ended up in bed with me. We talked and prayed about it. But just as her fears started creeping into her daytime activities as well, things started to get better. She seldom came to me during the night, and one day while changing her bed linens, I realized why. Written on a crumpled piece of paper under her right pillow I found the verse from 2 Timothy 1:7 (KJV): "God hath not given us the spirit of fear; but of power, and of love, and of a sound mind."

> *The source of the strength we need to endure the trials can largely be found before we ever enter the valley or winter of our lives.*

Ashley had conquered an unnecessary kind of fear, but healthy fear remained. She was able to sleep through the night knowing she was safe, but she still would not get into a car with a stranger or wander off by herself.

God doesn't want us to look to the future with fear but with hope. If you belong to God, difficulties belong to Him. He'll lead you safely through all things, and when you can no longer walk, He'll carry you. He will either shield you from suffering, or He will give you strength to bear it. Be at peace. Don't be anxious.

But also don't be unwise. Some people, like the grasshopper, choose to drink, sing, and dance in the summer instead of storing up for the winter. For those people, starving is almost eminent.

Similar suffering in two different people can lead to two different responses—some to self-destruction and others to new life. Those who look at suffering as a half-full glass and have taken the necessary steps to be prepared may even realize that necessity has pushed them where virtue never would have led them. Life's disruptive moments force us to rely on resources we may not know we have, so it's up to us to keep those resource reserves full when things are going well.

Work now, for "the night cometh when no man can work" (John 9:4 KJV). Healthy physical, emotional, and spiritual reserves will help us coast through the hard times and come out OK. Depleted reserves, on the other hand, can catch us unaware and leave us destitute. God loves and respects human freedom too much to free us completely from the pain involved in our journeys through life. Instead, He equips us through preparation and goes with us through them.

I spoke recently with my eighty-eight-year-old friend Lavina. She reminded me, as she often does, that she had gone up in an airplane with Orville Wright when she was seven. She's one of those people you just want to sit and learn from, be mentored by. Her joy is contagious, her life full. Yet she's known more than her share of suffering. She says she's been sick nearly every day of her life. Her husband "had his head blown off in a hunting accident." Yet she laughs lightly and talks about her many brushes with death. "I like to think God isn't ready for me yet because he hasn't found the cabbage rose wallpaper I want for my room in the mansion. You can only get that in Europe, you know." Her weak voice grows more serious. "God hasn't healed me, but He's given me the strength to go on despite the many problems."

I asked Lavina how she lived for the best while preparing for the worst, and this is what she said:

> I always realize who I am. I'm a child of the king. A king knows everyone in his court. [My king] knows what's going to happen to

> me. He will take care of me. He has a responsibility and so do I. My part is to obey in his court. His responsibility is to take care of me.

In her book *A Quiet Place in a Crazy World* (Multnomah 1994), Joni Eareckson Tada writes about the importance of forging a relationship with God while living for the best and preparing for the worst:

> When I was a little girl, I visited my Uncle Vincent's house on the eastern shore, near Easton, Maryland. One afternoon Uncle Vince took me upstairs to show me his "prayer room."
>
> I remember thinking, *This is strange. This is a little rigid. God ought to be meeting Uncle Vince on the golf course, like He meets me when I go horseback riding, or when I go hiking with Daddy. How odd that Uncle Vince needs this little room. . . .*
>
> But in later years, looking back, I found myself thinking, *How wise of Uncle Vince to have had a place all those years where he met Jesus.* That's probably the reason why he could pray on the golf course and when he went hiking with us. Uncle Vince encountered God every place . . . because he had one place. How we need such a place, a quiet place.

David found it. Job found it. Jeremiah found it. They found their quiet places with God while things were good. And it was in those quiet places they found strength to sustain them when things got bad.

Bible

We read about David in chapter 4. Let's revisit his life and discover the ways he knew how to live for the best while preparing for the worst by finding his quiet place with God wherever he was. It started in Bethlehem, where, as he guarded his sheep, he learned to sing praise songs and play his harp to the Lord. Then as David was anointed by the Spirit to become king, that same spirit left King Saul (1 Samuel 16:14–23). As a result, Saul became tormented by an evil spirit, which God permitted to come (v. 14). Saul could find relief only through music, so he commanded that a musician be found (vv. 15–17). In His providence, God arranged that David be the one, so the shepherd boy—who'd found his quiet place with God—was introduced to the palace and the king. And the Holy Spirit empowered David to drive away the evil spirit that overwhelmed Saul (v. 23).

Then David faced the Goliath challenge. David relied on the things he'd learned in the quiet places when he said, "Your servant has been keeping his father's sheep. When a lion or a bear came and carried off a sheep from the flock, I went after it, struck it and . . . killed it. . . . Your servant has killed both the lion and the bear; this uncircumcised Philistine will be like one of them" (1 Samuel 17:34, 36). And when Saul tried to get David to wear his armor, David said, "'I cannot go in these, . . . because I am not used to them.' So he took them off" (1 Samuel 17:39).

But David had tested his faith in God in the quiet places of his life. And that prepared him for the giant Goliath and the giant Saul, who would later try to kill him as well. In 1 Samuel 18 (NKJV) we read of David's responses through these hard places:

- Verse 5: he "behaved wisely"
- Verse 14: he "behaved wisely"
- Verse 15: he "behaved very wisely"
- Verse 30: he "behaved more wisely"

David was not only chosen from eternity to be founder of the messianic dynasty of kings, but he was also providentially prepared by the Lord to undertake his royal responsibilities. He had learned to play the harp, a skill that would make him sensitive to the aesthetic side of life and that would help him compose the stirring psalms that extol the Lord and celebrate His mighty exploits. David had been brought into the palace of the king as musician and warrior so that he might acquire the experience of statecraft. Though an uninitiated novice at the time of his anointing, he was eminently equipped to be king of Israel at his coronation some fifteen years later.

By living for the best (playing his music and learning to trust God in the shepherd's field), David was prepared for the worst (killing Goliath and running for his life from Saul for ten years). David walked closely with God in the good times, and because he did, God equipped him for what he'd need in the harder times. Like the ant in Aesop's fable, David somehow knew that they who drink, sing, and dance in the summer run a great risk of starving in the winter, for they're unprepared. David's healthy spiritual life in the quiet places sustained his physical life through the trials.

Application

The essence of the kingdom of God tells us that we make ourselves ready for the return of Christ by being born again and then living as His disciples. Once that's taken care of, God uses us in this age for His purposes in the age to come. All mankind faces trials, in fact, whether they're in or out of the kingdom. But as kingdom dwellers, particular struggles lie ahead, and we must be prepared. Here's how:

Pray. Be a prayer warrior before the battle begins. Find your quiet place in the morning or night. Spend time with God. Tell

Him what's on your heart, and listen to what He tells you. Like my dad said, praise Him when you're on the mountaintop so you'll be ready for the valley experiences.

Study. Know Scripture. Ephesians 6:11–18 tells us to arm ourselves with defensive weapons—truth, righteousness, peace, and salvation. The one offensive weapon this passage tells us to take up is "the sword of the Spirit, which is the Word of God" (v. 17). What do we do with this weapon? "Be alert [ready, prepared] and always keep on praying for all the saints" (v. 18). Unless we read God's Word regularly, listening daily to His voice, we aren't likely to hear Him when the roof caves in, when the winter comes. He doesn't usually speak when we open it up randomly.

Don't be afraid, be wise. Your tendency will be to become fearful. We always do when we face the unknown. But the Bible tells us to be "wise as serpents, and harmless as doves" (Matthew 10:16 KJV). Samuel didn't know what lay ahead of him, but he, like David, knew what lay behind. So he erected a stone memorial and named it Ebenezer, meaning "Thus far has the LORD helped us" (1 Samuel 7:12). You can erect your Ebenezer, too, then walk confidently into the future.

Fellowship. Hang with people who work like the ants to be ready for tomorrow. Many people, even Christians, live in this world as though they're going to stay here always. Many people don't prepare for difficulties that lie ahead—even Christians. They buy health and life insurance, convince them to also "buy" catastrophic insurance for the things that lie ahead.

Sing. Learn songs. Make up songs. Play praise music. Just learn to live with praise on your lips because you're ready and God's in control. Remember Jehoshaphat's song on the front line of war? Remember the songs David wrote and recorded in the Psalms while he was in the thick of battle? Again, He developed a song in his heart in the good times that spilled over into the bad.

Share. The surest way to make yourself ready for battle is to share your battle strategies of hope with others. "Why do you smile when you know what lies ahead?" Funny you should ask. We read in 1 Peter 3:15: "Always be prepared to give an answer to everyone who asks you to give the reason for the hope that you have."

Seek balance. Not too little, not too much. The right kind of fear, but not the wrong. Jesus sought to always be prepared by finding balance in His life, as evidenced in Luke 2:52: "And Jesus grew in wisdom and stature, and in favor with God and men." Jesus built His reserves intellectually, physically, spiritually, and socially, and these balanced reserves sustained Him through the battles.

If God is the answer through the smooth places, He's still the answer when trouble comes.

Understand that God never changes, only circumstances do. "Every good and perfect gift is from above, coming down from the Father of the heavenly lights, who does not change like shifting shadows" (James 1:17). If God is the answer through the smooth places, He's still the answer when trouble comes. Be ready, but don't sweat it.

Conclusion

I went to lunch recently with Andrea, a woman in her late twenties, who asked me questions about finding God's will for her life. She wondered about a possible marriage to the man she'd been seeing for some time. Andrea bemoaned the holding pattern in her life. "Nothing bad is happening. Nothing at all is happening. What do I do?" she said.

Sitting in my favorite Mexican restaurant, I glanced back in time. I described a period in my life when I asked the same questions. The only thing I *knew* to do was be a good mom and write. Today, some ten years later, my children are almost grown, and I have no regrets beyond my human weaknesses. And the writing, well, you be the judge. It was during those not-knowing-what-lies-next, but I-need-to-keep-going days, that I learned to rely on God. Someone had said to me, "Sit at His feet, Lynda. Learn who He is. There'll never be a better time than now." And she was right.

Job walked with integrity, blameless and upright before the Lord, in the good times as well as the bad (Job 1:1). Jeremiah found God's word's and "he ate them" (Jeremiah 15:16) through prosperity, and those truths sustained him through difficulties. David did his job in the field (1 Samuel 17:15), and developed a relationship and deep trust in the Lord through his quiet, uncelebrated battles. "Behaved wisely" are the words used four times about David. And somewhere in God's book, He's kept track of what Andrea and I talked about during *those* times to prepare us for *these* times. He wants to do the same for you. And if we do, if we live for the best while preparing for the worst, the reserves we'll need will be there.

Bible Study

Don't look to the future with fear but with hope. If you belong to God, difficulties belong to Him. He'll lead you safely through all things, and when you can no longer walk, He'll carry you. He will either shield you from suffering, or He will give you unfailing strength to bear it. Be at peace. Don't be anxious.

1. God is sovereign and deserves holy fear.

From Job, Job 28:28: "The fear of the Lord—that is

____________________________, and to shun evil is ____________________________.”

FROM DAVID, PSALM 19:9: “The fear of the LORD is pure, __________________ forever. The ordinances of the LORD are _________ and altogether righteous.”

FROM JEREMIAH, JEREMIAH 32:39–40: “I will give them singleness of heart and action, so that they will always fear me ______ ___________ _______ _________ and the good of their __________________ after them. I will make an everlasting covenant with them: I will never stop doing good to them, and I will inspire them to fear me, so that they will never turn away from me.”

2. *God is in charge, so we need not know unholy fear.*

PROVERBS 1:33: “But whoever listens to me will live in _____________ and be at ease, without fear of harm.”

1 JOHN 4:18: “There is no fear in love. But perfect love drives out fear, because fear has to do with ______________________. The one who fears is not made ________________ in love.”

3. *Because we have the ultimate kingdom of God to look forward to, we can have hope.*

ROMANS 15:13: “May the God of hope fill you with all joy and ___________ as you ___________ in him, so that you may overflow with hope by the power of the Holy Spirit.”

2 THESSALONIANS 2:16–17: “May our Lord Jesus Christ himself and God our Father, who loved us and by his grace gave us eternal encouragement and good hope,

___________________ your hearts and ________________ you in every good deed and word."

ROMANS 5:1–2: "Therefore, since we have been ___________________ through faith, we have peace with God through our Lord Jesus Christ, through whom we have gained access by faith into this __________ in which we now stand. And we rejoice in the hope of the glory of God."

HEBREWS 6:19: "We have this hope as an ____________ for the soul, firm and secure. It enters the inner sanctuary behind the curtain, where Jesus, who went before us, has entered on our ____________."

TITUS 2:13: "While we wait for the blessed hope—the glorious appearing of our great God and Savior, Jesus Christ, who gave himself for us to ____________ us from all wickedness and to purify for himself a people that are his very own, eager to do what is good."

Dear God:

Thank You that we can live for the best while preparing for the worst when we know You. As long as we walk closely with You on the mountaintops, You'll be right there with us through the valleys. And we don't have to live in fear but in hope for the future. But make me wise like the ant, and store up physical, emotional, and spiritual reserves for the harder times. David did it, and that made him ready for what lay ahead. I know that as long as it is day, we must do Your work, because night is coming when no one can work. Show me how to do that, Lord. In the name of Jesus Christ, amen.

You cannot cure your sorrow by nursing it;
but you can cure it by nursing another's sorrow.

—George Matheson

CHAPTER 9

The People

That we can comfort
those in any trouble with
the comfort we ourselves
have received from God.

—2 CORINTHIANS 1:4

I don't remember her name, but she sat on the front row of our Sunday school class on the left side. I'll call her Kathy, and she was in her late twenties. Everyone had dressed in their Sunday best, and our teacher had just finished greeting everyone and asking for praises and prayer requests. That's when Kathy stood quietly and faced the rest of us in the room. "I have something to say."

Kathy went on to describe how the day before, she'd gone with our church group to minister in the inner city. She'd been one of the ones on the street praying with people and urging them to come inside and eat. Kathy went on to say that she'd made a mistake and lit up a cigarette with one of the street people, trying to establish rapport. One of the older women in the group came running up to her and jerked the cigarette out of her mouth, scolding her loudly in front of the stranger, who turned and walked away.

I watched Kathy point to her hair, which had black roots and blond ends about halfway grown out. "My hair," she said, "not only represents its own growth but my growth as a Christian for the past six months." Kathy smoothed the dark roots. "This new growth represents the drugs and alcohol and immorality I no longer take part in."

Kathy wiped a tear and looked at us around the room. "But these blond ends still have a way to go. And so do I. Please be patient with me and others like me as we work our way through our own private pains."

TAKING THE TIME

I've never forgotten Kathy's words. They reminded me that the essence of suffering is to cause us to grow and then to help others do the same, to expand our world and help us reach into the world of others. George Meredith said, "There is nothing the body suffers that the soul may not profit by." Shelley says of poets, "They learn in suffering what they teach in song." We are called to persevere and find strength in our own suffering. Once we find more strength than we ever knew possible for ourselves, we are called to repeat that process in different people and in different situations. When I became a single mom, I did so scratching and clawing all the way. Little did I know that God would use my tears and experience to do the Focus on the Family magazine for single parents.

Once we find more strength than we ever knew possible for ourselves, we are called to repeat that process in different people and in different situations.

Pity or sympathy we feel for the sufferings and misfortunes of others and a desire to give help or show mercy is called *compassion. Sym-* means "with," *-pathy* is from *pathos,* meaning "pain" or "suffering." Suffering with one another, entering into the feelings of a sufferer. Sympathy and compassion are born in the womb of experience. In *Wishful Thinking* (HarperSanFrancisco, 1993), Frederick

Buechner writes: "Compassion is the sometimes fatal capacity for feeling what it's like to live inside somebody else's skin. It is the knowledge that there can never really be any peace and joy for me until there is peace and joy finally for you, too."

We cannot bless unless we bleed like Jesus did (Hebrews 2:9–18; 4:15). God has compassion. "The LORD is good to all; he has compassion on all he has made" (Psalm 145:9). And He wants us to have it too: "As God's chosen people . . . clothe yourselves with compassion, kindness, humility, gentleness and patience" (Colossians 3:12).

When we respond in the right way to our own suffering, we discover even in our moments of powerlessness that someone else is reaching to us. On the other hand, we can get so preoccupied with our own inconveniences in life, that we fail to even hear the cries of others asking for help, as illustrated in this conversation between Pooh and Eeyore in *Winnie the Pooh:*

> Pooh: "Did you fall into the river, Eeyore?"
> Eeyore: "Silly of me, wasn't it?"
> Pooh: "Is the river uncomfortable this morning?"
> Eeyore: "Well, yes, the dampness you know."
> Pooh: "You really ought to be more careful!"
> Eeyore: "Thanks for the advice."
> Pooh: "I think you're sinking."
> Eeyore: "Pooh, if it's not too much trouble, would you mind rescuing me?"

At other times, the method we use to reach the hurting, like Kathy, may be so off target that we fail to meet their needs. I found this to be true after my daughter left to live with her dad. I searched everywhere I knew for help during that time and failed to find anyone to understand. I took my family for visits to three counselors, none of whom could get to the bottom of what hurt. I went to our pastor's office the night she left and told him what had happened. One week went by, two weeks, three weeks, and I received no phone call or visit. I called individuals from our church for advice and prayer, but they didn't know what to do.

One particularly bad Friday for me, I saw the wife of one of the people from church I had called. She walked out of my office as I returned from a meeting. "Oh, how are you doing, Lynda.?" And I lost it. "Do you care? Does anyone care?" The woman followed me into a supply closet, where I sobbed and heaved. Finally the woman asked me to come to someone's home for dinner the next Monday night. I arrived to my designated seat at the head of the table with the pastor's wife on my left and this woman on the right. They proceeded to throw questions and suggestions at me, which seemed more like the condemnation I didn't need to hear. The mismatch of all the individuals who either tried and failed or didn't try at all to help me reminded me of a short story called "I Taught Them All," by Naomi White:

> I have taught in high school for ten years. During that time, I have given assignments among others, to a murderer, a pugilist, a thief and an imbecile. The murderer was a quiet little boy who sat on the front seat and regarded me with pale blue eyes; the pugilist lounged by the window and let loose at intervals in a raucous laugh that startled even the geraniums; the thief was a gay-hearted Lothario with a song on his lips; and the imbecile, a shifty-eyed little animal seeking the shadows.
>
> The murderer awaits death in the state penitentiary; the pugilist lost an eye in a brawl in Hong King; the thief, by standing on

> tip-toe, can see the window of my room from the county jail; and the once gentle-eyed little moron beats his head against a padded wall in the state asylum.
>
> All those pupils once sat in my room, sat and looked at me gravely across worn brown desks. I must have been a great help to those pupils. . . . I taught them the rhyming scheme of the Elizabethan sonnet and how to diagram a complex sentence.

I know now that the journey I went through with my daughter was one God used to help me change my perspective, understand the problem, yield to the process, identify the purpose, trust His provision, measure my progress, grow in my prayer life, and prepare for what else would come. But at that time, I felt more as though I'd been abandoned. And through that experience, I learned how difficult—and important—it is to say and do the right things at the right time for the right individuals before God, without messing with His work in that person's life.

God won't eliminate suffering for Kathy or you or me or cause pain to happen only to bad people. But God uses people—friends, neighbors, family—as salve to pour on the wounds of those who hurt. These people ease the burden and fill the emptiness and instill new hope and confidence in the sufferer. Remember Aaron and Hur? They held up Moses' tired hands during a battle against the Amalekites, bringing victory to Israel (Exodus 17:10, 12). They didn't take the battle away from Moses, they just lent their strength to help him work through it. When he saw they believed in him, Moses found it easier to believe in himself through his reliance on God. He stood stronger and taller with the help of the two men beside him.

Patsy Clairmont tells in her book *Normal Is Just a Setting on Your Dryer* (Focus on the Family, 1993), about cutting flowers from her garden. She explains that the stem of a cut flower seals the severed area to preserve the moisture it contains. But this self-protective action prevents the flower from taking in additional nourishment. In fact, florists tell us to make fresh cuts on the stems before setting cut flowers in water in order to extend their lives.

Patsy goes on to tell about a time when she discovered her sister's illness as she herself was going through an exceedingly difficult time. Then as if she had received a fresh cut, she went to be by her sister's side and in doing so, found new strength for herself. She writes, "I wasn't strong because of any special wisdom or stamina within myself, but because I had plunged into the water of the Great Sustainer." And because she did, Patsy found the strength to help others.

Our goal in helping others through suffering is to let them know everyone goes through hard times, and with Christ, they'll come out OK.

> There is no path
> So dark,
> Nor road so steep,
> Nor hill so slippery
> That other people have
> Not been there
> Before me
> And survived.
> May my dark times
> Teach me to help
> The people I love
> On similar journey.
> (Maggie Bedrosian, "No Road Too Steep")

Bible

Jesus modeled compassion wherever He went. Though He suffered more than you or I could ever know, He took time to feel the hurts of others. Condemned criminals and half-breeds and women of ill-repute and short guys with too much money. Jesus didn't care who it was, He just mastered compassion. Sometimes for those who followed Him, as in Matthew 14:14: "When Jesus landed and saw a large crowd, he had compassion on them." Other times He displayed compassion toward those who didn't follow Him, as in Luke 7:13 when He saw the unnamed widow who had just lost her only son: "When the Lord saw her, his heart went out to her."

We read about others in the Bible who also showed compassion. In Luke 15:20, a father felt compassion toward his prodigal son: "But while he was still a long way off, his father saw him and was filled with compassion for him." And the Samaritan in Luke 10:33 found it his job to minister to a perfect stranger lying in the street: "But a Samaritan, as he traveled, came where the man was; and when he saw him, he took pity on him."

Pity or guilt may cause us to pause and consider the plight of those less fortunate. But true compassion dresses Christlike love in working clothes. True compassion is always followed by action.

What did Jesus do when He felt compassion for the crowds? He healed their sick. What did He do with His compassion for the bereaved widow? He said, "Don't cry," and He went on to minister to her. When the father felt compassion for his son, "he ran to his son, threw his arms around him and kissed him" (Luke 15:20). And the good Samaritan put his compassion to work when "He went to him and bandaged his wounds, pouring on oil and wine. . . . and took care of him" (Luke 10:34).

We would have a better shot at consistent compassion if we'd remember that in another place, another time, any one of us could easily be that homeless person. Ours could be the children begging on the street. A pastor of ours told how in southern Florida, he lived only an hour and a half plane ride north of Haiti, where his life expectancy would be only forty-five. Less than two hours' distance added an average of thirty-five years to a person's life.

We would have a better shot at consistent compassion if we'd remember that in another place, another time, any one of us could easily be that homeless person. Ours could be the children begging on the street.

Every day, we should show compassion to others in our words as well as our deeds. Go beyond emotion. Give your last dollar to the man on the street corner. Send monthly support to the orphan. As Jesus pointed out, "Shouldn't you have had mercy on your fellow servant just as I had on you?" (Matthew 18:33).

APPLICATION

One of the things God has accomplished through my oldest-daughter struggles is to help me learn how to help others through their difficult times. What went right with my own help along the way, and what went wrong? And from those experiences, what have I learned about making a difference in the loads people are called to bear without impeding the growth of their spiritual muscles?

DON'T

Don't try to rescue the sufferer. Each person must walk through his or her own hard places. My neighbor Nan started calling me a number of years ago to discuss her marital problems. A stay-at-home-mom, Nan had gotten involved with a man on the Internet. Though nothing more came of the two-month relationship, the event uncovered other problems between Nan and her husband and triggered a five-year struggle in their marriage. When she'd come to my house and cry, my impulse was to remove the pain. Instead, I guided her to God's Word to find immediate answers to struggles they faced. Just two days ago, I touched base with Nan to find out how things were going. "We've had a six-month honeymoon. Things are going great!"

Remember learning about the chrysalis—the pupa of a butterfly? The cocoon phase provides the butterfly-to-be with a sheltered place for growth. It pushes, swells, and convulses in order to break through to freedom. I have known of people who have tried to help the process along by snipping the remaining restraints for the butterfly. But that retards the growth process, and often the butterfly dies. The observer was only trying to help, but she didn't know that while the pupa struggles to free itself from its constraints, it adds color to its body and strength to its wings. I often think of this analogy when I'm tempted to rescue my children or people like Nan from their dilemmas. When I do, I thwart the process of bringing strength and color to their character. Don't rescue. Let the growth process finish its course.

Don't expect the sufferer to feel your passion and beliefs. God knew we'd fight this urge while helping others. You and I have learned our passion for God in the hard places, the wildernesses, and so should the sufferer. "It was not your children who saw what he did for you in the desert until you arrived at this place. . . . But it was your own eyes that saw all these great things the LORD has done" (Deuteronomy 11:5, 7). One morning as I drove my kids to school, a Christian song came on the radio that I loved. It talked about the return of Jesus. "Oh, guys, listen. Isn't that beautiful?" I turned to watch one yawn and the other draw in the vapor on the window. The words meant more to me because of my wilderness experience, where I'd found God faithful. My children hadn't been there yet.

Don't assume you can do nothing to help. This passage in Deuteronomy goes on to say, "Teach them [God's Words] to your children, talking about them when you sit at home and when you walk along the road, when you lie down and when you get up" (Deuteronomy 11:19). I've tried to use this principle with my children for many years by teaching godly concepts to them as issues and opportunities arise—in the car, before bed, at the dinner table. God presents opportunities to teach them ways to navigate through tough places. You'll be responsible for recognizing the times. But never expect your children or neighbors or friends to feel the same passion for God that you do. You learned yours in the wilderness experience; so will they. Your job is to help encourage them through it. In her book *Give Them Wings* (Focus on the Family, 1994), Carol Kuykendahl writes, "Don't prepare the road for the child. Prepare the child for the road."

Don't think that the sufferer will forget God as soon as she's away from the pain. Deuteronomy 6:10–12 assures us that God is at work in their lives in all kinds of ways. "When the LORD your God brings you into the land . . . a land with large, flourishing cities you did not build, houses filled with all kinds of good things you did not provide, wells you did not dig, and vineyards and olive groves you did not plant—then when you eat and are satisfied, be careful that you do not forget the LORD, who brought you out of Egypt, out of the land of slavery." Don't expect the sufferers to inherit your passion, but keep telling them the truth, when they lie down and when they rise up. Meanwhile God is working on them in other ways, such as people and circumstances. You're not the only one involved in helping this person.

Don't try to accomplish huge tasks. Do small things with great love. "Write them [God's word's] on the doorframes of your houses and on your gates, so that your days and the days of your children may be many in the land" (Deuteronomy 11:20–21). During my struggle with my daughter, other than prayer, sometimes the things I could do seemed minuscule, such as a phone call or note. On several occasions when I would return to that area to speak, I'd drive down to see her. Other times, I'd use frequent-flyer miles and fly her or one of my other children with me to spend one-on-one time. Small things with great love. That's all God called me to do.

Don't think the sufferer automatically knows how to suffer well. "Remember how the LORD your God led you all the way in the desert these forty years, to humble you and to test you in order to know what was in your heart, whether or not you would keep his commands" (Deuteronomy 8:2). Carol came to me after I taught my Sunday school class, asking me if she could come to my house that afternoon and talk. Besides preparing for my class, I had finished writing the narration for the Easter cantata and substituted for the children's pastor during worship service. I needed rest and to spend time with my family. So after my afternoon nap, I loaded my son in the car with his bicycle and met Carol at a nearby park.

We walked as Clint rode, and Carol talked about all her concerns. I listened to them, one at a time. Then I modeled for her how to give them to God. Two people, eyes open as they walked around Sharon Woods Lake, touching the throne of God. When we returned to my car, I wrote what we'd done on the back of a deposit slip and handed it to her. I hope I taught her *how* to fish (or pray) rather than just handing her a fish that day. You learned the hard way; so will they. There are no vicarious processes.

Don't assume you've arrived at maturity. Because you feel compassion doesn't mean you've arrived. It just means you're moving in the right direction. God can show His own compassion to any willing vessel yielded to His work. My son, Clint, felt compassion for a neighbor boy whom I scarcely noticed. I found him doing little things to encourage this boy who knew nothing about spiritual things. God will put people to help—and receive help—through the lives of his children, no matter what their ages.

Don't blame the victim. Sometimes if we blame the one who suffers for his or her own misfortune, evil doesn't seem quite so irrational and threatening. In turn, we tend to believe that the good things we enjoy we also deserve. It's not a matter of luck. "If the woman didn't dress so provocatively, she wouldn't have been assaulted." "If she worked harder, she wouldn't be so poor." This kind of rationalization makes everyone feel better except the victim. They, instead, feel doubly abused through the original misfortune and through social condemnation.

Don't remain distant or keep quiet. When you don't know what to say after tragedy or pain has struck someone you know, don't decide to excuse yourself. When you are active in a local body of believers, when you support your local church and pastor, and when you pray for Christian ministries, you will soon find problems and ways to help. But don't forsake your friendships, pack your bags, and walk off. You don't abandon a true friend when he has problems; you stay and pray with him. We need to develop this character in our churches, prayer fellowships, and ministries, so that our brothers and sisters do not suffer needlessly. Send a card, make a phone call, drop by for a visit—just let them know you care. We must not only share the compassion of Christ, but do something about it, as He would.

Don't do all the talking. Listen with your heart as well as the mind. The hurting person probably doesn't want a sermon. She wants someone to take the time to listen and understand and cry with her. Be available. Be supportive. Be real. Be quiet. Listening, it's probably the most important thing you can do when someone has signaled to you for help.

Don't try to help in your own strength. Every day, talk to God about opportunities you will have and how you should respond. Ask for wisdom, He'll give you lots of it.

Conclusion

Kathy stopped coming to our church in Ohio shortly after visiting our Sunday school class. I don't know what her hair or her Christian growth looks like today. But I do hope that somewhere she is maturing in the Lord. I pray that she found someone more willing to take the time to suffer with her through her hurts and growth. We've all been in the shoes of Kathy as well as the older woman who made a wrong call that day. Let's agree to make a change now. Be deliberate about your availability to those who hurt. God is watching, and so are they.

Bible Study

Jesus gave us the example for helping others. It begins with compassion and ends with follow-up action. If you don't take the time to feel compassion for those who hurt, you won't need any other skills or wisdom. But learning to feel the hurts of others is a God-given gift. Begin your quest for others-ministry, by asking God for compassion.

1. Compassion is where it starts—or ends.

ROMANS 12:15: "Rejoice with those who rejoice; mourn with those who mourn."

1 PETER 3:8: "Finally, all of you, live in harmony with one another; be sympathetic, love as brothers, be compassionate and humble."

Where can you show more compassion?

____

2. Whom to show compassion toward:

- The unbeliever

JOB 6:14: "A despairing man should have the devotion of his friends, even though he forsakes the fear of the Almighty."

- The chastened

JEREMIAH 9:1: "Oh, that my head were a spring of water and my eyes a fountain of tears! I would weep day and night for the slain of my people."

- The enemies

PSALM 35:12–13: "They repay me evil for good and leave my soul forlorn. Yet when they were ill, I put on sackcloth and humbled myself with fasting."

- The poor

PROVERBS 19:17: "He who is kind to the poor lends to the LORD, and he will reward him for what he has done."

- The weak

GALATIANS 6:2: "Carry each other's burdens, and in this way you will fulfill the law of Christ."

- The believers

1 CORINTHIANS 12:25–26: "So that there should be no division in the body, but that its parts should have equal concern for each other. If one part suffers, every part suffers with it; if one part is honored, every part rejoices with it."

To whom can you show more compassion?

____

3. *Seven things to say to someone in pain:*
   - God sees our pain and takes our loss seriously (John 11:36; Matthew 23:37; Isaiah 40:1).

   - Every life is a complete life (Psalm 139:16).

   - God loves little children and welcomes them all to Him (Matthew 19:14; 2 Samuel 12:23).

   - God has a purpose we can't understand (Isaiah 55:8–9; Deuteronomy 29:29; 1 Corinthians 13:12–13).

- We are part of the fallen human race. C. S. Lewis wrote, "Wars don't cause death. Wars simply hurry the process for some people." All of us die, it's just a matter of when.

- People closest to God have never been immune to pain (1 Peter 3:18).
  What can you do or say today to demonstrate compassion?

  ____

Dear God:

We've all seen it done wrong, and we want to do it right. You tell us to comfort those in any trouble with the comfort we ourselves have received from God. Instill compassion in us this day, then fill us with wisdom on how to respond with actions. Put people in my path today to help, and show me what to do. I don't know how, but You do. Thank You for Your example. In the name of Jesus Christ, amen.

O Captain, my captain our fearful trip is done.
The ship has weathered every rack, the prize we sought is won.

—Walt Whitman, "O Captain, My Captain"

CHAPTER 10

The Payoff

Strengthening the souls of the disciples, exhorting them to continue in the faith, and saying, "We must through many tribulations enter the kingdom of God."

—ACTS 14:22 NKJV

I carried in my hammer and screwdriver and got to work, moving gently around the antique frosted cathedral-style glass. The door had hung in the house since it was built in the 1920s. Shortly after graduating from college and working at my first teaching job, I had purchased the fixer-upper, one-time nursing home to use as a rental. I wondered how the glass in the door had survived all the activity through the years as I pried the stuck hinges, removed the door, and carried it out to my '66 Mustang convertible.

I drove back to my apartment and stored the door under my bed. I was engaged to be married in a few months, and I got excited about using the door in just the right place in my home. Well, the wedding happened, but before I could hang the door, the man I married left, and the location of my home changed. I wrapped the door in a quilt and moved it with me and my three children to another state, where I began my doctoral program.

The door landed first in our apartment and then in the home we purchased. I had all kinds of ideas for what I'd finally do with it. But one day I received the call to move to Colorado. I lugged the door up the basement stairs at our Ohio home and carried it to the westbound truck. The door quickly found a place in temporary storage of our unfinished basement. I would later decide how I would use it. I thought, *Surely I'm "home" this time.* But I soon found that would not be the case.

Full Circle

I began this book by telling you about the difficulties my daughter encountered after we moved to Colorado. I'll end this book by telling you she's not quite there yet, but she's well on her way. And so's her mom, who went out seeking relief from her pain but found, instead, a deeper relationship with the One who would walk with her through it. In the process, this mom's become a greater kingdom seeker and a person who looks a little more like Christ. And it happened through pain. I know that now. So did Amy Carmichael when she wrote:

> It is only the very ignorant, or those who do not see what they read, who can forget that almost all the pages of every true book of history, and most true biographies, even of those which tell of a search after truth in one or other of the worlds of thought and action, are stained blood-red; and if one thinks at all, the heart-racking thought will not be refused, it is not past; it is going on—"groaneth and travaileth in pain together until now."

What, then, is the answer to why we hurt? I believe the best we can understand with our human thinking is we hurt so we can keep our minds on heavenly things. If the kingdom of heaven reminds us of the ultimate inheritance to those who trust God,

> *If the kingdom of heaven reminds us of the ultimate inheritance to those who trust God, pain serves as a reminder of what to avoid.*

pain serves as a reminder of what to avoid. You won't be able to completely understand why your baby died or your sister suffered rape or your family faced financial ruin until you see Him, who endured the Cross and bears the scars on His hands, feet, and side. Then we will understand, even as all along we have been understood.

But until then? What does a child do whose mother or father allows something to be done—pulling a tooth or receiving a spanking—which he or she cannot understand? These acts hurt for the present, but they yield a greater good down the line. So far down the line, in fact, that the child can't see it. That's when he or she learns to trust. It's the only way of peace, and the only way I've chosen to go.

When I look out ahead at what could happen in the future to me or my family, I just trust. I call it the "scarlet assurance." Moses understood it when he put the scarlet blood on the lintel and doorposts of Israelite homes so devastation and death would not visit them (Exodus 12). They escaped destruction. Rahab also demonstrated her scarlet assurance. In Joshua chapters 2 and 6, she hid the Israelite spies in Jericho in exchange for the protection of her family. She tied a scarlet cord in the window so destruction would pass them by. And it did. Another woman, known only as the mother of Lemuel, looked ahead at what could happen, and she lay hold of that scarlet assurance: "When it snows, she has no fear for her household; for all of them are clothed in scarlet" (Proverbs 31:21). I've covered myself and my home with scarlet too. So even when the snow flies, everything's going to be OK.

When we have proven God good past telling, we trust and find rest there.

What a place to stay. When we have proven God good past telling, we trust and find rest there. The faith of the child rests on the character it knows. So does ours, and eventually we'll get the bigger picture. Today's spanking can mean tomorrow's discipline. Today's denial can mean tomorrow's plenty. Today's sorrows may mean tomorrow's glory. God's provisions are God's gifts to us. How we use them is our gift to Him. We just trust and keep on going.

KEEP GOING

Persevering isn't easy. I ran 10K races in my younger days. The race itself was difficult, and it required lots of discipline and training to stay in shape. But it's those times when things happened to me—pulled muscles, inclement weather, tired body—that made the feat seem impossible, and I wanted to drop out of the race. I remember such an event one June Saturday in Indiana. I was six weeks pregnant, had a sprained right ankle, and the rain fell in sheets. But I made up my mind to keep going. I persevered. Finishing became my goal, regardless of the fact that I crossed the end line something like 150 out of 175. But I did finish.

> When things go wrong, as they sometimes will,
> When the road you're trudging seems all uphill,
> When the funds are low and the debts are high
> And you want to smile, but you have to sigh,
> When care is pressing you down a bit,
> Rest! If you must—but never quit.
>
> Success is failure turned inside out—
> The silver tint of the clouds of doubt—
> And you never can tell how close you are,
> It may be near when it seems afar;
> So stick to the fight when you're hardest hit—
> It's when things seem worst that you mustn't quit.
> (Author unknown)

Keep going, it's worth it. You can persevere by doing the Peter Rabbit thing and becoming continuous wheelbarrow standers. This will allow you to keep your eyes not only on what's around you, but on what lies ahead. The kingdom now, and the really big one that will come later. And the Bible tells us to get rid of anything that hinders us from crossing that finish line into the greatest of all kingdoms:

> Throw off everything that hinders and the sin that so easily entangles, and let us run with perseverance the race marked out for us. Let us fix our eyes on Jesus, the author and perfecter of our faith, who for the joy set before him endured the cross, scorning its shame, and sat down at the right hand of the throne of God. Consider him who endured such opposition from sinful men, so that you will not grow weary and lose heart. (Hebrews 12:1–3)

The Kingdom of God Now

Why persevere? During Jesus' ministry, the kingdom of God is spoken of always as a future event. It is expected, hoped for, and prayed for. But it is never said explicitly to have arrived, not even at the Last Supper. What is present is the agent of the kingdom of God, Jesus, as we discussed in chapter 2. And what was Jesus' role?

- Jesus, the one who would usher in the kingdom into the present was already here.
- The reign of God over His people was performed through Jesus' teaching.
- Through Jesus, the kingdom of God became a timeless reality.
- Jesus became an agent of the kingdom of God.

- Jesus made the kingdom of God so imminent, that it came virtually here, though still in the future—already but not yet. An advance, but not quite the full presence of the kingdom of God.

- Jesus' healings and answered prayers evidenced the fact that the kingdom of God was at hand, happening now.

British theologian C. H. Dodd writes, "The absolute other has entered into time and space. The inconceivable had happened: history had become the vehicle of the eternal; the absolute was clothed with flesh and blood." In Jesus' person and actions the future was already realized since He who was to usher in salvation at the end was already present.

In chapter 1 we talked about how changing your perspective is the place to begin. The kingdom of God has been changing perspectives ever since Jesus' time. A political kingdom, in which the Jewish nation, under their Messiah, would rule the world—that's what they were expecting. Herod shared that notion, and tried to destroy Jesus in childhood, because he thought that Christ's kingdom would be a rival political kingdom to his own. John the Baptist understood Jesus' kingdom to be political as well, and when He gave no indication of being that kind of king, John began to doubt whether Jesus was the Messiah after all (Matthew 11:3). The twelve apostles also believed in a political kingdom until after the resurrection. The last question they asked Jesus was, "Lord, are you at this time going to restore the kingdom to Israel?" (Acts 1:6). Their minds were on political independence for their country, rather than personal eternal salvation.

But the kingdom Jesus came to give was not a political kingdom, but a kingdom that would reign in the hearts of men and women who dared to change their perspectives and accept the abundant life Jesus came to bring. That's why we can look up to Him in the midst of our pain and find new *perspective* and a better grasp on the *problem* of pain. That's why we can recognize the *process* of growth taking place in us through the things we're called to suffer. That's when God's *purpose* begins to emerge, and we can acknowledge that His *provision* never fails. At that time you can measure your *progress* as a kingdom grower and gain a deeper understanding of *prayer's* role through the pain. This will help you *prepare* for future disruption, and help you teach other *people* to do the same.

And the best part about the kingdom is, this isn't the best part.

The Kingdom of God Then

The more you allow God to establish His kingdom in your heart, the more you realize what's to come. The harbinger. The foretaste. The down payment we talked about in chapter 2 that leads to what scholars call the *consummation*—the payoff. *Consummation* is defined as the ultimate end, the act of becoming complete in every detail. Heaven will not only be more than we can imagine, but that more will go on forever. Timeless ecstasy forever. "No eye has seen, no ear has heard, no mind has conceived what God has prepared for those who love him" (1 Corinthians 2:9). And for now, every good pleasure on earth is but a shadow of its fulfillment in heaven.

For now, every good pleasure on earth is but a shadow of its fulfillment in heaven.

That's why you and I can enjoy things like my antique door now. God intersperses our lives with good things. If I like the frosted glass now, just think what I'll get later!

Those of us who have put our faith in the atoning work of Christ are said to possess eternal life, to be in Christ or to be saved, despite the fact that eternal life or salvation are essentially eschatological—or future—concepts. So also we as believers may be said to have entered into the kingdom of God despite the fact that the kingdom of God, like eternal life and salvation, can be properly experienced only at the end of time.

What Jesus began doing to sin won't be finished until His Second Coming, which will usher in the ultimate kingdom of God, and our purchase will be complete. Then we'll be able to understand all things, see things from the ultimate wheelbarrow. "Now we see but a poor reflection as in a mirror; then we shall see face to face. Now I know in part; then I shall know fully, even as I am fully known" (1 Corinthians 13:12).

In heaven you will see your husband, child, relative, friend—all live free from pain and struggle. You won't cry anymore. You'll see then how your perseverance through pain sent repercussions rumbling through the lives of people you didn't know were watching.

Your suffering, like nothing else, has prepared you to meet your Savior. To have shared in His suffering will fade like a half-forgotten dream" Weeping may have endured for the night (Psalm 30:5), but morning is on the way. And the joy will come.

Consider It Pure Joy

So buck up. "And I will give her her vineyards from thence, and the valley of Achor [trouble] for a door of hope: and she shall sing there" (Hosea 2:15 KJV). Author Joyce Meyers said, "Be content, happy, enjoy where you are while you're on the way to where you're going." God wants hearts burning with passion for future things, aflame with His hope.

Hope, like peace, is a sign we are managing our troubles fairly well. Joy is a sign that we are managing our troubles very well. Joy in death. Joy in disappointment. Joy in divorce. Joy in poverty. Trouble doesn't mean that joy will never visit us again, nor does joy mean that trouble will never visit us again. We'll get a little trouble in life and a lot of joy.

> *Trouble doesn't mean that joy will never visit us again, nor does joy mean that trouble will never visit us again. We'll get a little trouble in life and a lot of joy.*

I sometimes get weary thinking back at all the twenty years of disruptions in my life, some of them good, others devastating. If the door could talk, no doubt it would say how it wished I had left it to live in its original home.

But simplicity and comfort and ease would not be the case for the door or me—and Jesus warned us it would be so. But Jesus knew that people like the suffering man at the Gate Beautiful I spoke of in the introduction of this book would reach out and take what was being offered to him in the midst of the pain when Peter said, "In the name of Jesus Christ of Nazareth, walk" (Acts 3:6). That man could have withdrawn in fear, but instead he reached out and accepted the kingdom of God now. What about you?

Bible

You can see by reading this book how much I like stories. I like to tell them, read them, and listen to them. I guess that's why I like the parables Jesus taught. Parables are a sort of extended metaphor, comparison, or illustration of spiritual truths conveyed by comparing them to the ordinary. Within the gospel accounts of Jesus' life, we find seventy-six different sayings about the kingdom of heaven, 103 including the parables.

Jesus used parables, in part, as dark sayings, with apparent double meanings to conceal for a time what He had to reveal. The kingdom that Jesus intended to establish was so utterly different from what was commonly expected of the Messiah, that it was necessary for Him to be tactful. So He used these stories to illustrate the origin, development, mixed character, and consummation of the kingdom, which to us seem clear, but were enigmas to the hearers of Jesus' day. In Matthew 13:3–9, we read one of Jesus' stories, which tells about the different kinds of people who would hear the kingdom-of-heaven message contained in this book:

> A farmer went out to sow his seed. As he was scattering the seed, some fell along the path, and the birds came and ate it up. Some fell on rocky places, where it did not have much soil. It sprang up quickly, because the soil was shallow. But when the sun came up, the plants were scorched, and they withered because they had no root. Other seed fell among thorns, which grew up and choked the plants. Still other seed fell on good soil, where it produced a crop—a hundred, sixty or thirty times what was sown. He who has ears, let him hear.

Jesus tells us here that different people will receive the good news of the kingdom in different ways. Some won't even listen. Some will accept it, but soon fall away. Some will hold on longer, but gradually lose interest. And some will grab hold in varying degrees to final fruition. I call the different kinds of receivers:

The Not-at-Alls
The Temporaries
The Little Bits
The Takers

As I draw this book to a close, I feel my motherly instincts surface. I've shared so many truths on these pages, and with all my heart I want you to grasp them. You don't have to beg or be a cripple anymore, even when life has dealt you a bad hand. Instead, you can reap the benefits of the kingdom of God that Jesus brought for you. Which will you be in receiving that truth today? A Not-at-All, a Temporary, a Little Bit, or a Taker?

Application

Jesus wanted so much for the disciples to understand the gravity of what He was saying, that He went on to elaborate on His story of the sower in Matthew 13:18–23. Consider what He said and plug the details into your own life.

The Not-at-Alls

> When anyone hears the message about the kingdom and does not understand it, the evil one comes and snatches away what was sown in his heart. This is the seed sown along the path. (v. 19)

The Not-at-Alls relegate the pathway to spiritual and emotional freedom into a vague dimension. "So what are you trying to say?" a Not-at-All crippled man might have said, then gone right on begging as the seed of truth died by the wayside.

The Temporaries

> The one who received the seed that fell on rocky places is the man who hears the word and at once receives it with joy. But

> since he has no root, he lasts only a short time. When trouble or persecution comes because of the word, he quickly falls away. (vv. 20–21)

The Temporaries might read this book and get excited about the truth it offers, then do nothing to put the truths into practice. "Hot dog!" the Temporary crippled man might have said. "But I haven't walked for a really long time." Then he would sit back down in his begging spot.

The Little Bits

> The one who received the seed that fell among the thorns is the man who hears the word, but the worries of this life and the deceitfulness of wealth choke it, making it unfruitful. (v. 22)

The Little Bits selectively take away some of the value of spoken truth and reject others. The Little Bit crippled man might have listened to others who said, "You can't possibly walk." By doing so, he might have stood only, and never found faith enough to walk and jump and praise God.

The Takers

> But the one who received the seed that fell on good soil is the man who hears the word and understands it. He produces a crop, yielding a hundred, sixty or thirty times what was sown. (v. 23)

The Takers reach out and grab every bit of the free gift being offered to them. This would describe the Taker crippled man we read about in Acts 3. Never again would he beg or remain a cripple. Because in the name of Jesus Christ of Nazareth, he rose up and walked.

Conclusion

Some people write from the end of the experience looking back. They tell you to hang in there. It worked for them, it'll work for you. Me? I'm just a fellow traveler like you en route to a city out ahead, whose builder and maker is God (Hebrews 11:10). But I've learned a lot, enough to keep me walking and jumping and praising God, despite occasional pains I experience. And from the depths of my heart, I can join in chorus and tell you that everything's going to be all right—for me and for you no matter what happens—because of what the Lord has done.

My lovely door is probably destined never to be hung as I pursue, instead, life's unexpected twists, turns, and detours. An antique dealer delivered my door back to our home just the other day. Weary of carting and storing the beautiful piece, I had given it to him to sell. But when he couldn't get what I knew it was worth, I had him bring it back.

I'll probably take another glance at the door one day when I leave it behind for the final time. That trip to live with Christ forever will deliver me to my permanent home at last. The door will be long forgotten as I walk on streets of gold and finally set down my roots in that pain-free, struggle-free, disruption-free home where I'll live forever. Won't you join me?

Bible Study

In Colossians 1:13–14, we read: "He [God] has rescued us from the dominion of darkness and brought us into the kingdom of the Son he loves, in whom we have redemption, the forgiveness of sins." The remarkable thing about this passage is that the transferal is described as an act already accomplished, as realized within the life of the believer. What will you need to incorporate into your life in this age?

1. *Perseverance*

   2 Timothy 4:7: "I have fought the good __________, I have finished the ________, I have kept the _________. Now there is in store for me the crown of righteousness, which the Lord, the righteous Judge, will award to me on that day—and not only to me, but also to all who have longed for his appearing."

   Acts 20:24: "I consider my life worth nothing to me, if only I may finish the race and complete the ________ the Lord Jesus has given me—the task of testifying to the gospel of God's grace."

   Hebrews 12:1–3: "Therefore, since we are surrounded by such a great cloud of witnesses, let us throw off everything that ______________ and the sin that so easily __________________, and let us run with perseverance the race marked out for us. Let us fix our eyes on Jesus, the author and perfecter of our faith, who for the joy set before him endured the cross, scorning its shame, and sat down at the right hand of the throne of God. Consider him who endured such opposition from sinful men, so that you will not grow weary and lose heart."

PHILIPPIANS 3:12–14: "Not that I have already obtained all this, or have already been made ______________, but I press on to take hold of that for which Christ Jesus took hold of me. Brothers, I do not consider myself yet to have taken ________ ____ ____. But one thing I do: Forgetting what is ____________ and straining toward what is __________, I press on toward the goal to win the prize for which God has called me heavenward in Christ Jesus."

ROMANS 8:17–18: "Now if we are children, then we are heirs—heirs of God and co-heirs with Christ, if indeed we share in his sufferings in order that we may also share in his __________ . I consider that our present sufferings are not worth comparing with the glory that will be ________________ in us."

1 PETER 1:6–7: "In this you greatly rejoice, though now for a little while, you may have had to suffer grief in all kinds of _________. These have come so that your faith—of greater worth than gold, which perishes even through refined by fire—may be _______ ________ and may result in praise, glory and honor when Jesus Christ is revealed."

2. Joy

JAMES 1:2–4: "Consider it pure joy, my brothers, whenever you face trials of many kinds, because you know that the testing of your faith develops perseverance. Perseverance must finish its work so that you may be _________ and __________, not lacking anything."

1 PETER 4:13: "But rejoice that you participate in the sufferings of Christ, so that you may be ___________________ when his glory is revealed."

JOHN 15:11: "So that my joy may be ____ you."

HABAKKUK 3:17: "Though the fig tree does not bud and there are no grapes on the vines, though the olive crop fails and the fields produce no food, though there are no sheep in the pen and no cattle in the stalls, yet I will rejoice in the LORD, I will be joyful in God my Savior."

Though my body is sick . . .
Though my relationships are suffering . . .
Though my plans have been thwarted . . .
Though my banking account is low . . .
Though . . .
Yet I will rejoice in the Lord, will be joyful in God my Savior.

3. *Age to come*
   - No death (Revelation 21:4)
   - No grief (Revelation 21:4)
   - No crying (Isaiah 65:19; Revelation 5:5)
   - Former things passed away (Revelation 21:4)
   - God will be in charge (Daniel 4:35).

Dear God:

We've reached the end of our journey through the question, God, Do You Care? *I started out wanting to know from a temporal perspective. Now I see things as You see them. Thank You for sending Your Son to make the kingdom of God a reality now. Help me persevere with joy in this age, as I look forward to my future inheritance in the age to come. Meanwhile, help me to use the things I've learned from what I've gone through to strengthen the souls of the disciples, exhorting them to continue in the faith, and saying, "We must through many tribulations enter the kingdom of God." In the name of Jesus Christ, amen, and amen.*